PENNSYLVANIA COLLEGE OF TECHNOLOGY LIBRARY

5 0608 01140687 2

GUIDE TO LEGAL RESEARCH
AND WRITING FROM THE
TRANSNATIONAL PERSPECTIVE

D1445629

GUIDE TO LEGAL RESEARCH AND WRITING FROM THE TRANSNATIONAL PERSPECTIVE

PROF. FRANCIS A. GABOR

VANDEPLAS PUBLISHING

UNITED STATES OF AMERICA

LIBRARY
Pennsylvania College
of Technology

One College Avenue
Williamsport, PA 17701-5799

APR 20 2009

Guide to legal research and writing from the transnational perspective

Gabor, Francis A.

Published by:

Vandeplas Publishing - June 2008

801 International Parkway, 5th Floor
Lake Mary, FL. 32746
USA

www.vandeplaspublishing.com

ISBN: 978-1-60042-040-5
© 2008 Francis A. Gabor

SUMMARY OF CONTENTS

ACKNOWLEDGMENTS

I would like to thank those individuals whose contributions enriched this book immensely. First, I thank the journals and authors whose works are reproduced herein: Mr. James H. Carter and *The Penn State International Law Review* for "Transnational Law: What is it? How Does it Differ from International Law and Comparative Law?," Prof. John C. Reitz and *The American Journal of Comparative Law* for "How to do Comparative Law," and Foundation Press for its permission to reproduce excerpts from *Comparative Law: Cases and Materials* (6th ed. 1998).

I also extend my thanks to the journals who originally published my own articles, excerpts from which appear in this book: *The Northwest Journal for International Law and Business*, *The Vanderbilt Journal of Transnational Law*, and *The Review of Central and Eastern European Law*.

Finally, I am deeply indebted to Tony Silva, my research assistant at the Cecil C. Humphreys School of Law, University of Memphis, not only for his dedication to this project but also for the extensive research he conducted and the editorial commentary he contributed to ensure its success.

I. FOREWORD

The twenty-first century global world order creates fundamental challenges for the American model of legal education. This professional model cannot focus only on one domestic legal system isolated from the rest of the world. American law students need a realistic exposure to a transnational legal perspective in the contemporary global legal environment.

This objective can be achieved in three stages. The first step requires a first year introductory course setting the foundation in public and private international law with the fundamental understanding of the comparative law methodology to grasp legal problems and institutions transcending through national boundaries. In the second stage, the transnational perspective should be emphasized in every domestic course, in the expanded coverage of public and private international law, and in the comparative law curriculum. Finally, in the third stage, law students should have the opportunity to apply their transnational learning experience by selecting an intellectually and professionally stimulating topic for academic research. Through this research, the student should focus not only on developing a thesis and writing a research quality seminar paper, but also on the potential for publication of the paper in law reviews and other legal journals.

This concise *Guide to Legal Research and Writing from the Transnational Perspective* can be used as a practical tool in the critical third stage of the transnational legal education process. Concise practical tips will assist students in the research and writing process. Samples of articles written by the author will provide a model for scholarly writing.

II. TRANSNATIONAL LEGAL PERSPECTIVE

1. *Transnational Law: What is it? How Does it Differ from International Law and Comparative Law?*

23 PENN. ST. INT'L L. REV. 797 (2004–05)

JAMES H. CARTER[*]

It is a pleasure for us at the American Society of International Law to co-sponsor this program on the important subject of transnational law. Charlotte has suggested that I begin by drawing from my personal experience, both educational and professional, to comment on the appropriateness of looking at law in transnational rather than international or comparative terms.

In this context, I can't resist beginning with Paul Simon's lines (from the song "Kodachrome"): "When I think back on all the crap I learned in high school, it's a wonder I can think at all." As this audience can imagine, I am tempted to substitute "law school" for "high school." I say that not because I was offered a poor education in international law. To the contrary, I was the beneficiary of a perfectly fine, traditional course in public international law. What I did find inadequate, even potentially misleading in terms of what I later experienced in practice, was a blinkered, purely domestic focus on U.S. civil procedure. My courses in that area all proceeded on the assumption that there was only one way to handle the procedural steps involved in dispute resolution, that which is found in U.S. courts; and my professors even assumed that a system such as our judicial process made

---

[*]Mr. Carter is President of the American Society of International Law and a partner of Sullivan & Cromwell, LLP in New York, NY, specializing in international dispute resolution.

3

procedural sense—a dubious assumption, I learned later. I think my education would have benefited from an infusion of an international prospective in this and other subjects.

Following a federal court clerkship, I began practice in 1970 and immediately found myself immersed in transnational disputes. Thirty five years ago, globalization was well underway. For example, I quickly found myself involved as a junior associate in disputes arising out of expropriation of copper mines in Chile and oil fields in Libya. The disputes involved parallel and sometimes inconsistent proceedings in the courts of several countries, as well as international arbitration proceedings. These matters included a combination of public and private international actors and legal principles and required the coordination of cases around the world in many different legal systems. All of this introduced me to such efficient, non-American litigation processes as written witness statements used in place of depositions and even in place of affirmative testimony at hearings.

I then became involved, and I have continued to be involved, in litigation in which parallel (or at least closely related) claims are asserted in the U.S. and in one or more foreign courts. Important issues here turn largely on comity and other judgmental factors.

I also have litigated problems involving international letters of credit (which are regulated by private industry customs and practices), transnational insolvency problems and trans-border merger and acquisition issues. Indeed, very little that I do involves problems that can be compartmentalized into the law of one nation alone.

My personal experience at a large law firm reinforces my view that we have all become transnational. A significant number of the new lawyers whom we hire each year at my firm were born outside the United States or are members of the first generation of their families born here. Many have useful language skills and significant transnational "life experience." We hire significant numbers of lawyers who were educated in Canada and elsewhere and have received LLM degrees in the U.S. but have had their fundamental legal training elsewhere. There are difficulties and risks involved in this, but we find that the language skills and other abilities that such lawyers bring to bear worth the effort.

Charlotte also has asked that I comment on organizations, other than the American Society of International Law and the Association of American Law Schools, of course, that can be seen to be considering issues of transnational law. First among these in my experience are the organizations that are developing law on an ongoing basis through transnational networks of largely private actors. This occurs in the world of international commercial arbitration, and more particularly in the case of international sports disputes. There, in the last ten years the Court of Arbitration for Sport, based in Lausanne, has led the way in developing a "lex sportive" that is followed by the sports federations that comprise the Olympic movement and that is respected and to some degree employed by domestic courts in various countries.

Two documents created just within the past year are good examples of a developing body of transnational arbitral principles—though not particular to sports disputes. Neither is statutory "law," but each is likely to be given significant weight when the issues to which it relates arise in domestic courts. The first of these is the American Arbitration Association/American Bar Association "Code of Ethics for Arbitrators in Commercial Disputes," a document first promulgated in 1977, widely cited by courts, and modified significantly and issued in a new edition in 2004 to encompass more completely international commercial disputes.[1] The second is the International Bar Association's "Guidelines on Conflicts of Interest in International Arbitration," which addresses disclosure requirements for arbitrators in transnational disputes.[2]

There are many other organizations working on similar transnational projects. For example, the American Law Institute and UNIDROIT recently published their "Principles and Rules of Transnational Civil Procedure."[3] Other ALI projects of a transnational nature include currently ongoing works entitled "Intellectual Property: Principles Governing Jurisdiction, Choice of Law and Judgments in Transnational Disputes" and the "International Jurisdiction and Judgments Project.[4]

The American Bar Foundation also addresses the internationalization of legal values and legal practices through numerous projects. Two among those currently pending involve "Globalization of Insolvency Lawmaking" and "Legal Professionalism and the Transformation of the Field of Legal/Business Advice" (focusing on multi jurisdictional practice issues).[5]

---

[1]AMERICAN ARBITRATION ASSOCIATION/AMERICAN BAR ASSOCIATION, THE CODE OF ETHICS FOR ARBITRATORS IN COMMERCIAL DISPUTES (2004), at http://www.adr.org; see Bruce Meyerson and John M. Townsend, *Revised Code of Ethics for Commercial Arbitrators Explained,* DISPUTE RES. J. (Feb./Apr. 2004) at 10.

[2]INTERNATIONAL BAR ASSOCIATION, IBA GUIDELINES AS CONFLICTS OF INTEREST IN INTERNATIONAL ARBITRATION (2004), *available at* http://www.ibanet.org/ images/downloads/ guidelines%20text.pdf.

[3]THE AMERICAN LAW INSTITUTE, ALI-UNIDROIT PRINCIPLES AND RULES OF TRANSNATIONAL CIVIL PROCEDURE (Proposed Final Draft March 9, 2004).

[4]Current ALI projects are listed at http://www.ali.org.

[5]Current areas of research are described at http://www.abf-sociolegal.org/currentAR/index/html.

Finally, Charlotte suggested that I offer a view regarding possible content for such a course in transnational law. It is perhaps bold for a practitioner to address an academic audience on how best to structure a course. Nevertheless, I did note the following course description a few months ago from the catalogue of one (anonymous) law school:

> Introduction to Transnational Law: It will teach students the minimum that every lawyer should know about the international dimensions of law in the modern world. . . . The course will cover both the public and private dimensions of transnational law. Among the topics to be studied are the law of treaties; customary international law; trade law; international environmental law; international criminal law; international tax law; international business transactions law; law on the use of force; transnational litigation; and transnational arbitration.

This sounds like a course that I would have been delighted to have had available to me as a student, but I wonder whether it does not try to cover too much. In a review essay this past year in the *American Journal of International Law,* Professor David Bederrnan discussed the latest crop of U.S. international law casebooks, noting how they now tend to stretch to add various elements of private, typically transnational law to the traditional public international law curriculum.[6] Conversely, this transnational law course description suggests that courses entitled "transnational" also find it necessary to include substantial elements of public international law.

I think it may be asking too much to put all of this in a

---

[6]David J. Bederman, *International Law Casebooks: Tradition, Revision, and Pedagogy,* 98 A.J.I.L. 200 (2004).

single course. I was glad to have had a good course in public international law in my student days. I could have used a separate course in transnational law to stand beside it. But perhaps more important, I also would have appreciated, in my law school days, the infusion of a transnational perspective into courses generally.[7]

---

[7]The University of Michigan, among others, takes such an approach. *See* Mathias Reimann, *From the Law of Nations to Transnational Law: Why We Need a New Basic Course for the International Curriculum*, 22 PENN ST. INT'L L. REV. 397 (2004); Panel, *International Law and the Legal Curriculum*, 96 ASIL PROC. 54 (2002).

2. *Stepchild of the New Lex Mercatoria: Private International Law from the United States Perspective*

8 NW. J. INT'L L. & BUS. 538 (1988)

FRANCIS A. GABOR[*]

I. INTRODUCTION

On December 11, 1986, at the United Nations Headquarters in New York, the United States deposited its instrument of ratification of the 1980 United Nations Convention on Contracts for the International Sale of Goods. With the ratification of the United States, Italy, and the People's Republic of China, the Convention became effective on January 1, 1988. While this culmination of a century-long effort by legal experts and merchants of the world community revitalizes the ancient *lex mercatoria* (law of the merchant), it also presents the challenge of its implementation in transnational legal practice.

It is anticipated that the ratification by the United States will accelerate acceptance of the Sales Convention by other nations. The large number of signatories and the drafting history, reflecting sophisticated compromises between diverse jurisprudential and socioeconomic views, are also encouraging signs for worldwide ratification.[1] Despite an opti‍mistic prognosis for the Convention's future, however, it is quite likely that a substantial number of countries will not join

---

[*]Professor of Law, Memphis State University. D.Jur. 1967, Eotvos L. Science University (Hung.), J.D. 1975, Tulane University, LL.M. 1974, University of California, Berkeley.

[1]Winship, *The Scope of the Vienna Convention on International Sales Contracts,* in INTERNATIONAL SALES: THE UNITED NATIONS CONVENTION ON CONTRACTS FOR THE INTERNATIONAL SALE OF GOODS 1-1 (N. Galston & H. Smit eds. 1984) [hereinafter INTERNATIONAL SALES].

it in the next decade. Private international law,[2] therefore, will still be needed for guidance in a decentralized transnational legal environment and will continue to be relevant in achieving unification and legal security.

Article 1(1)(b) of the Sales Convention relies on the rules of private international law of the potential forum in an attempt to extend its scope of application. The United States (along with several other countries) ratified the Convention subject to a reservation to Article 1(1)(b), adopting the position that the Sales Convention applies only if both contracting parties have their places of business in countries that ratified the Convention. The unsettled and unpredictable status of private international law prompted this limitation. Private international law rules of a non-signatory nation cannot lead to application of the Sales Convention when a United States citizen is a party to a transnational contract with a citizen from a non-signatory nation.[3] Under United States law, therefore, either the Uniform Commercial Code ("U.C.C."), or the relevant foreign commercial law apply in a sales context, unless both contracting parties are from Convention states.

Due to the United States limitation, a critical goal remained even after ratification of the Sales Convention: unification of the choice of law rules applicable to the

---

[2]Private international law refers—in United States terms—to international conflict of laws. This term includes: 1) judicial jurisdiction; 2) recognition and enforcement of foreign judgments; and 3) choice of law to be used in resolving a transnational legal conflict.

[3]The major purpose of this reservation is to prevent the unexpected application of the Sales Convention. For example, the choice of law rules of the forum can refer to the application even if only one of the contracting merchants or neither of them have their business establishment in a State which ratified the Sales Convention. This would occur if the law of a contracting state were chosen as controlling, and the law of that nation accessed the Sales Convention.

international sale of goods. This objective was achieved in a unique joint conference of the United Nations Commission on Unification of International Trade Law ("UNCITRAL") and the Northwestern Hague Conference on Private International Law. The joint conference prepared the Hague Draft Convention on the Law Applicable to Contracts for the International Sale of Goods, which takes great strides toward resolving legal and socioeconomic differences among the world's trading nations.[4]

This Article briefly assesses the potential implementation of the Hague Draft Convention from the standpoint of the United States interest in the worldwide unification of international trade law and concludes that United States interests would be well served by adoption of the Hague Draft Convention.

II. LACK OF SEPARATE PRIVATE INTERNATIONAL LAW IN THE UNITED STATES

Private international law developed in Europe as a result of the gradual disintegration of the *ius commune* founded on the Roman law.[5] As private laws gradually became "nationalized" by emerging nation-states, and finally codified, private international law became a unique guiding and harmonizing legal force through its uniform Roman law heritage. The principle of national sovereignty set the foundation for the creation of rules of private international law, and a unique body of domestic laws developed which provided solutions for international jurisdiction and choice of law problems.

It is not surprising that the founder of United States conflict of laws, Justice Joseph Story, relied on the well-

---

[4]The Hague Draft Convention is reprinted as an appendix to this Article.

[5]*See generally* 1 E. RABEL, THE CONFLICT OF LAWS: A COMPARATIVE STUDY 1-48 (1960).

developed European traditions of private international law in his *Commentaries on Conflict of Laws*,[6] which transplanted the European tradition to United States soil. As the complex federal system developed in the nineteenth and early twentieth centuries, conflict of laws primarily served the interests of the United States interstate system; the truly international cases and problems suffered relative neglect.[7]

In the present era, the absence of one well-developed body of private international law engenders substantial uncertainty and legal insecurity for both United States and foreign citizens contemplating transnational legal relationships.[8] The lack of a separate body of private international law in the United States presents a major issue in attempts at international unification of laws applicable to the international sale of goods.

Since the United States ratified the Sales Convention subject to reservation, implementation in the United States will begin with a restrictive approach. Rules of private international law will be disregarded as a source leading to the application of uniform law. At this time, it is critical for United States interests to reassess the significance of a unique separate body of private international law applicable to international sales of goods.

It is well recognized that in the United States, the international conflict of laws basically includes: 1) judicial jurisdiction over foreign defendants; 2) choice of law; 3) international judicial assistance and co-operation; and 4) questions of recognition and enforcement of foreign country judgments. Lack of a uniform and separate body of laws governing international conflict of laws problems has inhibited

---

[6]J. STORY, COMMENTARIES ON THE CONFLICT OF LAWS (8th ed. 1883).
[7]*See E.* SCOLES & P. HAY, CONFLICT OF LAWS 8-34 (1982).
[8]*Id.*

United States ability to participate effectively in the international unification process thus far. The ratification of the Sales Convention presents a fresh opportunity for progress in internal unification of United States rules of private international law.[9]

One of the most burning problems for the United States in this decade is its sliding performance on the world markets. The staggering trade deficit calls for effective legislation by the United States Congress to secure greater protection for, and performance of, United States industries within the legal framework of the General Agreement of Tariffs and Trade.[10] While this work is progressing on the domestic law and public international law levels, the private transactional aspects of international trade should not be neglected. The unsettled status of international law on the level of the private transaction acts as a unique "non-tariff barrier" to international trade. Thus, it is critical that the United States make significant progress toward the harmonization and eventual unification of private laws and in particular, private international law governing the international sale of goods. The United States ratification of the Sales Convention signifies progress in this direction.

III. RECOGNITION OF PARTY AUTONOMY

As long as the United States does not have a separate codified or harmonized body of rules dealing with private international law, the most effective legal safeguard for United

---

[9]Gabor, *Emerging Unification of Conflict of Laws Rules Applicable to the International Sale of Goods: UNCITRAL and the New Hague Convention on Private International Law*, 7 Nw. J. INT'L L. & BUS. 696, 699-700 (1986).

[10]For an excellent and comprehensive discussion by leading authorities, see Symposium, *U.S. Trade Policy: Problems and Options*, 18 N.Y.U. J. INT'L L. & POL. 1075 (1986).

States transnational contracts however, recognize that in the majority of the cases, the place of delivery will be the state where the seller has its domicile or principal place of business. Therefore, Article 191 frequently leads to the application of the seller's law. On the other hand, the law of the buyer's domicile or place of business will usually be applied, in the absence of an effective choice of law by the parties, if the delivery of the contract takes place in that state.[11]

The most important question for analysis is whether the prevailing United States approach to choice of law in the international sale of goods manifested in Article 191 and Article 188 of the *Restatement (Second)* can be effectively reconciled with the unification rule set out in Article 8 of the Hague Draft Convention. Article 8 contains a sophisticated compromise at its core: "To the extent that the law applicable to a contract of sale has not been chosen by the parties in accordance with Article 7, the contract is governed by the law of the state where the seller has his place of business at the time of completion of the contract.[12] Accordingly, in the absence of choice of law by the parties, the law of the seller's principal place of business shall govern."

The rationale for this choice of law rule lies in the legal and socio-economic foundations of the international sales contract. In a typical case, the seller bears the more complex and demanding performance in the transaction. The seller's range of obligations are, in relative terms, less precisely defined. Moreover, the seller faces more uncertainty in the transnational environment in the course of fulfilling contractual obligations. Therefore, the seller's reliance on the seller's own legal system to govern all aspects of the transnational contract contributes a great deal towards

---

[11]*Id.* comment f and illustrations.
[12]Hague Draft Convention, art. 8(1).

certainty, uniformity, and a sense of legal security.[13]

The prevailing United States approach under the *Restatement (Second)* does not distinguish between domestic and transnational contracts. The majority of United States cases nonetheless reach a result comparable to that of Article 8(1) of the Hague Draft Convention, favoring the law of the seller. On the other hand, the exceptions to the basic premise form the core of the Hague Draft Convention. The major shift from the law of the seller's state to the application of the law of the buyer's state is found in Article 8(2):

> The contract is governed by the law of the State where the buyer has his place of business at the time of conclusion of the contract, if—(a) the negotiations were conducted, and the contract concluded by and in the presence of the parties, in that state; or (b) the contract provides expressly that the seller must perform his obligation to deliver the goods in that state; or (c) the contract was concluded on terms determined mainly by the buyer and in response to an invitation directed by the buyer to persons invited to bid (a call for tenders).[14]

The three major exceptions in Article 8(2) reflect the legal and socioeconomic interests of buyers in international sales transactions. Most of the developing countries supported these exceptions in order to shift the balance in favor of the possibly economically weaker buyer.[15] The first exception has a narrow scope of application. It disregards to some extent

---

[13]M. PELICHET, *supra* note 8, at 85-91. *See also* Jaffey, *The English Proper Law Doctrine and the EEC Convention,* 33 INT'L & COMP. L.Q. 531 (1984): Lipstein. *Characteristic Performance—A New Concept in the Conflict of Laws in Matters of Contracts for the EEC.* 3 NW. J. INTL'L & BUS. 402, 406-07 (1981).

[14]Hague Draft Convention, art. 8(2).

[15]Hague Convention Minutes, *supra* note 25, INTERVENTION NOS. 5-10.

the realities of modern international trade in since both negotiation and signing of the contract do not typically take place in the buyer's state.

The second exception is more controversial, and its impact more substantial. It refers to the law of the place where the seller delivers the goods according to the terms of the contract. This exception requires characterization of the essential elements of contract performance by the potential forum and, as long as there are no uniform laws in effect on this point, this exception creates uncertainties in the application of the Hague Draft Convention.[16]

The most controversial provision of the Hague Draft Convention, however, lies in Article 8(3), which establishes the general "escape clause" from the application of Articles 8(1) and 8(2).

> By way of exception, where in light of the circumstances as a whole, for instance, any business relations between the parties, the contract is manifestly more closely connected with the law which is not the law which would otherwise be applicable to the contract under paragraphs 1 or 2 of this Article, the contract is governed by that other law.[17]

The adoption of this clause generated heated debate among the delegates to the Hague Draft Convention. Many of the civil law countries, including the socialist countries, strongly opposed this clause, emphasizing that it would create an inherent and dangerous uncertainty in the effective application of the Hague Convention. The delegates of the civil

---

[16] *See* Travaux Prepartoire, in HAGUE CONVENTION MINUTES NO. 7 OF COMMISSION I: INTERVENTION NOS. 20-21 (1985). The final vote reflected a lack of compromise on this exception as seventeen delegates voted in favor of it, sixteen delegates voted against it, and fourteen delegates abstained from voting.

[17] Hague Draft Convention, art. 8(3).

16

law countries, relying on their legal heritage, emphasized the need for clearly defined a priori choice of law rules as the basic foundation for creating international legal security in this area.

At the same time, most of the common law countries, including the United States, placed more weight on the need for practical flexibility in determining the private international law governing the sale of goods. The delegates from common law countries insisted that a general escape clause, such as Article 8(3), forms a necessary part of the overall compromise to work out effective and uniformly recognized choice of law rules dealing with the international sale of goods.[18]

The Article 8(3) escape clause of the Hague Draft Convention clearly expresses the United States interest manifested under *the Restatement (Second)* and other modern approaches to conflict of laws.[19] It is well recognized in the United States that Article 191 of the *Restatement (Second) is* a presumptive choice of law rule only, which can be replaced by application of a policy-oriented analysis under the general principles of Article 188. The most significant relationship test of the *Restatement (Second)* can thus be viewed as a discretionary escape for United States judges. Thus, the general escape clause of the Hague Convention is quite

---

[18]*See* Gabor, *supra* note 9, at 718-19.

[19]*See generally* Currie, *The Verdict Quiescent Years*, 28 U. CHI. L. REV. 258 (1961); Currie, *Conflict, Crisis and Confusion in New York*, 1963 DUKE L.J. 1; 3 A. EHRENSWEIG & E. JAYME, PRIVATE INTERNATIONAL LAW (spec. pt. 1977); Kegel, *Paternal Home and Dream Home: Traditional Conflict of Laws and the American Reformers*, 27 AM. J. COMP. L. 615 (1979); Nadelmann, *Impressionism and Unification of Law: The EEC Draft Convention on the Law Applicable to Contractual and Non-Contractual Obligations*, 24 AM. J. COMP. L. 1 (1976). *But see* Zweigert, *Some Reflections on the Sociological Dimensions of Private International Law or What is Justice in the Conflict of Laws?*, 44 U. COLO. L. REV. 283 (1973) (This article was published in German as *Zur Armut des internationalen Privatrechts an sozialen Werten*, 37 RABELSZEITSCHRIFT 435 (1973)).

consistent with the modern United States choice of law methodology; it can be easily adopted by the United States. The crucial question remaining, however, is whether the United States choice of law system *effectively* governs interstate legal relationships in its constitutionally coordinated federal system, where the semi-sovereign states share common legal traditions. The federal system permits and necessitates legal flexibility. On the other hand, the decentralized transnational legal environment has 185 sovereign legal systems each relying on its own unique national legal traditions. Whether the same level of flexibility and uncertainty can be easily adopted in this diverse landscape, remains uncertain.

***

V. PROPOSAL FOR IMPLEMENTATION OF INTERNATIONAL UNIFORM LAWS

A. The Sales Convention

Revitalization of the ancient *lex mercatoria* is one of the major achievements of our century. The creation of a uniform substantive law applicable to the international sale of goods eliminates a major non-tariff barrier to the free flow of goods and services across national boundaries. The United States has a vital interest in becoming an active participant of this process, as evidenced by its ratification of the Sales Convention. The next phase of the unification of international trade law is the challenge of implementing the new rules on international and national levels. On the international level, the most important United States interest lies in the promotion of global participation in unification. The present signs are quite encouraging. The drafting history and the large number of signatory states point to a potential worldwide ratification of the Sales Convention.[20] A major stumbling block for effective implementation lies in the unsettled status of private international law, caused in part by the United States and other countries' reservations to the Sales Convention.[21]

The effective implementation of uniform laws should be based on consistent interpretation of their essential provisions. The most effective measure to achieve this goal is the creation of a central authority for interpretation of the new uniform laws. One successful example of this method is provided in the protocol adopted to the Brussels Convention on Jurisdiction and Judgments,[22] which gave jurisdiction to the European Court of Justice over interpretation. A similar protocol is attached to the new Rome Contractual Obligations Convention,[23] establishing uniform choice of law rules for contracts among citizens of the member states of the European Economic Community. A similar central authority obviously cannot be easily established in the more diversified

---

[20] *See* Winship, *supra* note 1, at 8-10.

[21] Sales Convention, U.S. reservation to art. 1(1 X6).

[22] Brussels Convention, *supra* note 46.

[23] The Rome Contractual Obligations Treaty, *supra* note 55, incorporates a joint declaration providing:

The Governments of the Kingdom of Belgium, the Kingdom of Denmark, the Federal Republic of Germany, the French Republic, Ireland, the Italian Republic, the Grand Duchy of Luxembourg, the Kingdom of the Netherlands, and the United Kingdom of Great Britain and Northern Ireland, On signing the Convention on the law applicable to contractual obligations; Desiring to ensure that the Convention is applied as effectively as possible; Anxious to prevent differences of interpretation of the Convention from impairing its unifying effect;

Declared themselves ready:

1) to examine the possibility of conferring jurisdiction in certain matters on the Court of Justice of the European Communities and, if necessary, to negotiate an agreement to this effect;

2) to arrange meetings at regular intervals between their representatives.

world wide community of nations. Perhaps a more reasonable approach would be designation of a court or arbitration tribunal for potential binding, or at least advisory interpretive authority over the Sales Convention.

A more feasible alternative would be to establish a digest for the regular publication of leading national court and arbitration decisions relating to the Sales Convention. Such a publication would promote consistent national implementation and interpretation of the Convention. A status table of the relevant ratifications with reservations and the significant scholarly and expert assessments of the leading provisions and cases could also be included in this comprehensive digest.[24]

On a national level of implementation of the new *lex mercatoria,* the United States should focus on its complex federal system. The Sales Convention was ratified by the United States as an international treaty; therefore, under Article VI of the United States Constitution it is the binding law of the land. The Sales Convention is a self-executing treaty which does not require further legislative enactment.[25] Accordingly, it is to be hoped that United States courts and arbitration tribunals will give a consistent interpretation of this convention and that the leading cases will be published in an appropriate form.

B. The Hague Draft Convention

At the same time, United States private international law applicable to the international sale of goods requires prompt action on federal and state levels. The long-term United States interest would be best served by federal legislation in this area. Congress has the constitutional power

---

[24]Gabor, *supra* note 9, at 726.
[25]*See generally* M. McDougal, H. Lasswell & J. Miller, The Interpretation of Agreements And World Public Order (1972).

to enact such legislation under the enabling legislation section of article IV, paragraph I, of the full faith and credit clause, but has never utilized its power in this area. The overwhelming majority of conflict of law problems have been left for the individual states in the federal system. At this stage of international unification of commercial law, however, it is critical that the United States "speak in one language" with the rest of the world. Reliance on the conflict of law systems of fifty states creates a sense of uncertainty and confusion in transnational commercial relation-ships. The *Restatement (Second)'s* modern policy-oriented approaches to judicial and legislative jurisdiction can function effectively within a federal system where the Constitution and the common legal heritage present a strong cohesive force among the member states. The same rules and approaches, however, can be self-defeating and confusing if applied in a transnational context. Thus, the creation of order in the form of a federal unification is an essential step forward in the effective implementation of the new *lex mercatoria* in the United States.

If a federal level of unification of international conflict of laws can-not be accomplished in the immediate future, another alternative for harmonization at the state level could be explored. The National Conference on Uniform State Laws can be used as an effective vehicle to implement unification of private international law. The commissioners of uniform state laws can draft model legislation on subjects where state legislation might help implement international treaties of the United States, or where world unification would be desirable.[26]

The Hague Draft Convention could serve as an

---

[26]*See generally* HANDBOOK OF THE NATIONAL CONFERENCE OF COMMISSIONERS ON UNIFORM STATE LAWS AND PROCEEDINGS OF THE ANNUAL CONFERENCE MEETING IN ITS NINETY-SECOND YEAR 220-47 (1983).

acceptable basis for legislation extending the application of U.C.C. Section 1-105. Article 26 of the Hague Draft Convention particularly takes into consideration the interest of federal systems,[27] and uniform legislation is the preferred form of implementation of the Hague Convention in the United States. Such legislation might take several years of experimentation on the state level before being universally adopted, but the United States is free under Articles 26 and 29 of the Hague Draft Convention to make selective reservations and suggest revisions based on experience in its federal system. The U.C.C.'s Permanent Editorial Board should carefully consider and analyze the Hague Draft Convention for adoption as model legislation. Realistic national unification through this vehicle can contribute to the elimination of the non-tariff trade barrier of legal diversity, and promote our free competition on the world market.[28]

VI. CONCLUSION

In sum, United States interests would be well served by its legal adoption of the Hague Draft Convention, thus far a neglected stepchild of the new *lex mercatoria.* The core choice of law provisions of the Hague Draft Convention can be reconciled with the prevailing United States judicial and arbitration practices under the U.C.C. and the *Re-statement (Second).* The scope of U.C.C. Section 1-105 could be extended to uniformly implement the Hague Draft Convention in the United States.

It is premature to assess the future international reception of the Hague Draft Convention, however. The widespread ratification of the Sales Convention will

---

[27]Hague Draft Convention, art. 26.
[28]Lando, *Contracts,* in 3 INTERNATIONAL ENCYCLOPEDIA OF COMPARATIVE LAW 3-8 (1976).

significantly influence this process. In the meantime, national choice of law solutions will be applied, which, according to Professor Reese's comment on this Article,[29] quite frequently will lead to comparable substantive results. Thus, the common underlying principles of different national approaches may lead the world trading nations to accept the unavoidable compromises manifested in the Hague Draft Convention.

---

[29]Reese, *Commentary*, 8 Nw. J. INT'L. L. & BUS. 570 (1988).

3. *How to Do Comparative Law**

46 AM. J. COMP. LAW 617 (1998)

JOHN C. REITZ

Still, the beautiful can be distinguished from the common, the good from the mediocre...

Each writer finds a new entrance into the Mystery, and it is difficult to explain.

Nonetheless, I have set down my thinking as clearly as I am able.

Lu Chi, from "Preface" to Wen Fu:
The Art of Writing 9 (Sam Hamill tr., 1987).

What do we teachers and scholars of comparative law tell our students when they ask for guidance on how to write a comparative law seminar paper, note, or comment? How do we respond to colleagues who say they are interested in using the "comparative law method" but want to know what it is? When we are asked to evaluate comparative law scholarship, what standards do we apply? Like most fields of legal scholarship, we do not have an official canon of great works for writing in the field to emulate. Is there even really a "comparative law method"?[1] If there is, does it need an overhaul in light of the persistent criticism that comparative law as a field of

---

*Reprinted with permission of the author and the *American Journal of Comparative Law*.

[1]Some leading comparatists have maintained that there is. *E.g.,* RUDOLF B. SCHLESINGER ET AL., COMPARATIVE LAW 2–52 (6th ed., 1998); 1 KONRAD ZWEIGERT & HEIN KUMOTZ, INTRODUCTION TO COMPARATIVE LAW 28–46 (Tony Weir tr., 2d ed. 1987).

intellectual endeavor has failed to live up to its promise?[2]

I believe that there is a "comparative method" and that it continues to offer strong benefits for the study of law. Most of us who teach and write in the field of comparative law, however, were not taught formally how to do comparative law. Rather, we have for the most part worked out our own methods based on an amalgam of the scholarship we thought effective for our particular purposes at the time. Moreover, we keep adjusting our approach for every new task. Some would see this self-taught experimental approach as a strength of the field. It may be a bit inefficient for every scholar to make up his or her own method, but no promising avenue will be barred by orthodoxy. However, as I have tried to answer the types of questions raised at the outset, I have come to wonder whether, despite the prevalent methodological agnosticism, there isn't really a large degree of consensus about the essentials of the comparative method. Perhaps we even have a canon.

In the hope of stimulating a discussion that might lead us to a clearer statement of that consensus, I offer the following nine principles about comparative law scholarship and the closely allied field of foreign law. The first principle considers the relationship between the study of comparative law and the study of foreign law. The next four principles (Nos. 2-5) concern the basic technique of comparing law in different legal systems and the special value of that type of study. There follow three principles (Nos. 6-8) concerning specific guidelines for carrying out a comparison involving legal subjects. The

---

[2] *See, e.g.*, MARTIN SHAPIRO, COURTS: A COMPARATIVE AND POLITICAL ANALYSIS vii (1980); Ewald, *Comparative Jurisprudence (I): What Was It Like to Try a Rat?*, 143 U. PENN. L. REV. 1889, 1891–93, 1961–65 (1995) (citing a number of other critical articles as well) *Frankenberg, Critical Comparisons: Re-thinking Comparative Law*, 26 HARV. INT'L L.J. 411 (1985).

final principle concerns the attitude which I believe to be indispensable for good comparative work. While I am interested in providing guidance in order to strengthen the quality of comparative law studies and increase interest in the field, I think it important to concede that there is no simple recipe for good scholarship. I am simply trying to list the most important characteristics of good comparative scholarship, with the caveat that deviations may always be made for good cause.

Basic Principles of the Comparative Method

1.

Comparative law involves drawing explicit comparisons, and most non-comparative foreign law writing could be strengthened by being made explicitly comparative.

The first clause of this principle may seem to verge on tautology, but it is amazing how much writing about foreign law is not explicitly comparative and yet is thought of as part of comparative law. I wish to insist that the comparative method involves explicit comparison of aspects of two or more legal systems. Some may object that any description of foreign law is implicitly comparative because all descriptions of foreign law are at a minimum trying to make the law of one system comprehensible for those trained in a different system. But I reject that argument on the grounds that the step of actually drawing the comparison is crucial to realizing the intellectual benefits of comparison. Actually framing the comparison makes one think hard about each legal system being compared and about the precise ways in which they are similar or different. If one wishes to claim the benefits of the comparative method, one cannot leave the act of comparison to the reader.

The foregoing statement is not meant to denigrate the

value of scholarship focused solely on foreign law. Indeed, all comparative law scholarship has to start by introducing some aspect of foreign law in order to have something to compare. The field of comparative law certainly depends on the study of foreign law and legal systems, so I do not want to suggest that the study of foreign law on its own terms cannot be a valid form of legal scholarship. See Section 7 infra. But I do mean to distinguish it from comparative scholarship.

I will also go so far on behalf of comparative law to argue that much "pure" (that is, non-comparative) foreign law scholarship could be made stronger by incorporating explicit comparison. The first argument has to do with strengthening the effectiveness of foreign law writing. Whatever other purposes a study of foreign law may be intended to serve, at a minimum it is no doubt intended to communicate to a domestic audience some aspects of the foreign law. The domestic audience will inevitably compare what the author tells them about foreign law with what they know about their own legal system. The communication will therefore be much more effective if the author draws the comparisons for them by summarizing the most important similarities and differences. In so doing, the foreign law scholar can also prevent the reader from making miscomparisons based on ignorance of her own legal system. This danger is all the more likely if the audience includes people who are not educated as lawyers, as it often does in the case of foreign law studies.

The second reason concerns the question of the audience for foreign law, an even more acute problem for foreign law than most other legal writing. Without explicit comparison to the home country explaining the relevance of the foreign law for the domestic legal system, most domestic lawyers will have little interest in reading a piece about foreign law. There are, no doubt, exceptions. Perhaps some areas of foreign law are of such general interest and obvious importance that a non-comparative, foreign law article on those subjects will interest a general legal audience.[3] Moreover, there will always be groups of country specialists and general comparatists for whom specialized treatment of foreign law will be interesting. Indeed, foreign law articles, even if not comparative, are crucial for comparative law scholars because they permit them to expand the number of jurisdictions with which they work beyond those that use languages with which they are comfortable and to whose legal materials they have access. But beyond these small circles, there are not likely to be very many people who will be interested in a foreign law topic unless the writer explains its relevance for contemporary, domestic issues, and such an explanation necessarily requires some explicit comparison.

Finally, I would argue that, in view of the ways in which explicit comparison is especially likely to contribute to our understanding of law, it is a shame for someone to have made the effort to master the details of certain aspects of one or more foreign legal systems and yet not take advantage of that knowledge, which is a prerequisite for comparison, to try to get the benefits of the comparative method. I argue in Sections 4 and 5 that the benefits of explicit comparison are exciting analytical moves that carry the promise of interesting insights. I believe that the disappointment critics have expressed in comparative law is in large part based on the fact that so much writing in the field is either entirely non-comparative or at best only weakly comparative. It therefore naturally fails to

---

[3]Some years ago, for example, there was a great deal of discussion in the U.S. about Japanese "administrative guidance" and more recently there has been considerable interest in the sudden development of constitutional litigation in the formerly socialist countries and the explosion of case law on many controversial subjects such as the treatment of the claims for restoration of property nationalized by the Communists.

deliver on the promise of comparison. Foreign law scholars could thus help comparative law "bring home the bacon" by employing explicit comparison.

Of course, there are many degrees of comparativeness. While some writing may be thoroughly comparative, other scholarship may focus on the law or legal system of a particular foreign country and use explicit comparison to domestic law solely as a frame to make clear the significant ways in which foreign law differs from domestic law or the reasons why a domestic lawyer ought to be interested in the example of a foreign legal system. As long as it uses some explicit comparison, legal scholarship has an opportunity to realize some of the intellectual advantages of the comparative method, and it is more likely to realize those advantages the more thoroughly comparative it is.

2.

The comparative method consists in focusing careful attention on the similarities and differences among the legal systems being compared, but in assessing the significance of differences the comparatist needs to take account of the possibility of functional equivalence.

Comparison starts by identifying the similarities and differences between legal systems or parts of legal systems under comparison. However, in performing the basic comparative job of identifying similarities and differences, one has to consider the scope of comparison: What is going to be compared with what? Here the comparatist comes face to face with the enigma of translation. In one sense every term can be translated because there are things in each legal system that are roughly the functional equivalent of things in the other legal system. In another sense nothing can be translated because the equivalents are different in ways that matter at least for some purposes. At a minimum, generally equivalent

29

terms in each language often have different fields of associated meaning, like, for example, "fairness" and "loyaute."[4]

One is thus always in some sense comparing apples and oranges. For example, jurors in the common law tradition bear some functional similarity to lay judges in the civil law tradition, but there are important differences in the way they come to and fulfill their office, including the way in which they interact with the professional judges and the kinds of non-criminal cases in which they participate. Consideration is a very different requirement from causae. Nor is it uncontroversial to say that the civil law simply omits the requirement of consideration because, if one asks what functions the doctrine of consideration might be said to fulfill (channelling, cautionary, evidentiary, and deterrent) - even though it admittedly does not do a very good job of fulfilling those functions - one can see that both German and French law have doctrines that might be considered in some sense to do the same thing.[5]

Comparatists dispute vigorously among themselves how big a problem the lack of congruity is in general and with respect to specific areas of comparison. But I think there is a high degree of consensus that good comparative analysis should pay careful attention to the problem of equivalency by probing how similar and how different the aspects of each legal system under study are. A comparative study of the consideration doctrine in British, French, and German law that simply reported that neither French nor German law recognizes the doctrine without considering whether French and German law achieve some of the same purposes with other rules would simply be a very weak effort.

---

[4]George Fletcher gave this example during our seminar discussions.

[5]von Mehren, *Civil-Law Analogues to Consideration: An Exercise in Comparative Analysis*, 72 HARV. L. REV. 1009 (1959).

Thus a good comparative law study should normally devote substantial effort to exploring the degree to which there are or are not functional equivalents of the aspect under study in one legal system in the other system or systems under comparison. This inquiry forces the comparatist to consider how each legal system works together as a whole. By asking how one legal system may achieve more or less the same result as another legal system without using the same terminology or even the same rule or procedure, the comparatist is pushed to appreciate the interrelationships between various areas of law, including especially the relationships between substantive law and procedure.

As in all fields of intellectual endeavor, a healthy skepticism about the received wisdom concerning differences and similarities and a strongly self-critical approach toward one's own conclusions are useful tools. Do civil law countries really refuse in all cases to treat court decisions as a source of law or are there civil law analogues to stare decisis? Does the U.S. constitutional limitation of federal court power to "cases" and "controversies" really prevent all abstract review of the kind permitted in continental European systems? How similar are the offices of judge in different legal systems? Or the role of private attorneys in litigation or in counseling? In the end, few rules or legal institutions - maybe none - have precise equivalents in other legal systems, and yet there are many rules and institutions which are broadly similar or similar in some very important ways. Comparative analysis proceeds in the tension between these two extremes. Good scholarship should normally try to figure out the extent to which the differences identified in law or legal systems are significant because they affect the outcome or the nature of the process and the extent to which they do not.

Before leaving the discussion of the basic procedure of

comparing, we need to discuss one technical term, the tertium comparationis, which a number of well-known writers insist upon as an essential element of the comparative method.[6] This imposing bit of jargon refers to nothing more than the common point of departure for the comparison, typically either a real-life problem or an ideal. For example, as suggested above, a comparative study of the consideration doctrine might take a functional approach by asking how each legal system under study determines which promises to enforce. A comparative study of constitutional law might ask how and to what extent each country under study implements the ideal of the rule of law. In large measure, the notion of a common point of departure seems inherent in the process of comparison. Either one legal system has the same legal rule or legal institution as another, or it has different rules or institutions which perform the same function, or it provides different results for a particular problem, or it does not seem to address that problem at all. A diligent search for similarities and differences ought to encompass all of those possibilities, so one may simultaneously agree that the term is essential to the comparative method and question whether one needs the special term at all. Nevertheless, the term may be useful as a way of reminding ourselves to be clear about the point of or framework for comparison and to hold that point or framework constant until the comparison is completed. The term has further utility in underlining the importance of looking into the question of functional equivalence.

Finally, as the example of comparison to an abstraction or ideal shows, the term permits a richer, more complex understanding of comparison. Neither system is likely to

---

[6]*See, e.g.*, Zweigert & Kumotz, *supra* note 1, at 30; Vagts & Cappelletti, *Book Review [Review of Edward McWhinney, Supreme Courts and Judicial Law- Making: Constitutional Tribunals and Constitutional Review (1986)*, 82 Am. J. Int'l L. 421, 423 (1988).

conform to the abstraction or ideal entirely, and each system may conform to the abstraction or ideal in different ways. For example, one might compare the judicial office in various countries by reference to the ideal of the rule of law. No one country perfectly implements the rule of law, and the ways in which they differ are not necessarily functionally equivalent. But one can still study how the ways in which they conform to or depart from the ideal differ and how they are similar. The use of a tertium comparationis may thus permit a more complex comparison, but the essential comparative techniques are the same. One compares each country's legal system with the ideal, and then one compares the ways in which each legal system fulfills or departs from the ideal to investigate similarities and differences between or among them, always investigating the possibility of functional equivalence.

In using ideals as a common point of departure for comparison, one must be on guard against the natural human tendency to use without reflection the ideals of one's own system as the normative measure for systems that may not accept the ideal. For example, the rule of law is an ideal that developed first in Western Europe and the United States. Some would argue today that it enjoys nearly universal acceptance; others would dispute that it does, pointing out how its development is tied to the development of society, law, and forms of government in the West. Thus, if one wishes to argue that one legal system is better or more highly developed than another because it better or more fully institutes the rule of law, one should not only consider carefully the question of functional equivalence, but also confront directly the question why it is appropriate to apply the rule of law as a normative measure. Of course, ideals by their nature are meant to carry normative force, so the use of an ideal as a tertium comparationis will naturally be understood as a normative argument. Therefore, if the comparatist means the comparison with the ideal solely as an analytic exercise, he had better make his non-normative stance especially clear. If he means it as a normative argument, he had better consider whether it is justifiable to apply the ideal to the societies in question.

3.

The process of comparison is particularly suited to lead to conclusions about (a) distinctive characteristics of each individual legal system and/or (b) commonalities concerning how law deals with the particular subject under study.

What should the point of the comparison be? Comparative study of law can be undertaken simply to inform the reader about foreign law, perhaps for the practical purpose of facilitating an international transaction or resolving a conflict of laws problem. It may be part of a campaign of law reform. It may be part of a comparative study of human culture or part of a critical project aimed at exposing the way law masks the exercise of power. It can even be used to spoof legal scholarship.[7] There is no reason why comparative studies should be limited to any particular set of purposes. The comparative method is just a tool.

From the nature of comparative studies, as outlined in the foregoing section, however, it can be seen that comparative law naturally and primarily leads in two directions at once. Because comparison focuses on both differences and similarities, comparative law studies cast light on (1) the special or unique natures of the legal systems being compared and (2) their commonalities with respect to the issue in question. The first direction leads toward defining the

---

[7]*See, e.g.*, Yablon, *Judicial Drag: An Essay on Wigs, Robes and Legal Change*, 1995 WISC. L. REV. 1129 (with perhaps more serious purpose behind the spoof).

distinctive features of each legal system. The second direction leads toward appreciation of commonalities, maybe even universal aspects, of legal systems and insight into fundamental aspects of the particular legal issue in question. Thus a comparative study of contract enforcement in France and the United States should lead to both (a) an appreciation of distinctive aspects of French and U.S. law, respectively, and (b) an appreciation of some of the fundamental problems of enforcement of private agreements in an economy with significant market activity.

It is important to bear in mind that comparison by itself is at best a "weakly normative"[8] exercise. As every adolescent in U.S. society learns, there is some normative force in the statement, "Everyone else is doing it," or "Nobody else's family does that," but, as we parents immediately counter, "So what?" Comparison is a relatively weak basis for normative argument. Rather, it is a sign that hard thinking about the normative basis for the apparently deviant behavior or rule is in order. Thus comparative studies may uncover interesting ideas for domestic law reform, but in the end the case for adoption of a foreign model cannot rest on the fact that many other countries have the rule or legal institution. The argument for domestic law reform has to be made in terms of normative claims acceptable within the domestic legal system, and probably the foreign transplant will have to be modified in significant ways precisely because each legal system reflects an at least partially unique legal system.

Because of its indispensability for testing claims of universality with respect to law and legal systems, social scientists have been strongly attracted to comparative law. Martin Shapiro has claimed that it should be a chief purpose

---

[8]Gianmaria Ajani used this phrase in the course of our seminar discussions.

of comparative law to provide data for testing general theories about law.[9] It is, indeed, a very exciting use for comparative law. But comparative law is not a mere appendage of social science. It is part of the general study of law, and therefore at heart, part of the humanities, like philosophy and history. Just as the social sciences may make use of philosophy and history, so too, they may make use of comparative law, but there are also many other important uses for comparative studies. The simple educative function of helping lawyers from one system understand and communicate effectively with lawyers from another system seems to grow more important every day as human transactions become ever more "globalized." For the same reason, there is renewed interest in efforts to harmonize law, in part by finding the "common core" of different legal systems' rules governing particular areas, like contracts, property, and torts. The spread of human rights discourse drives a similar interest in the "common core" of public law in order to help define, in the weakly normative way discussed above, what the ideal of the "rule of law" should mean. In all of these activities, the basic comparative method leads us to commonalities, simultaneously relativizing differences and correcting overhasty generalizations by revealing distinctive differences, as well.

4.

One of the benefits of comparative analysis is its tendency to push the analysis to broader levels of abstraction through its investigation into functional equivalence.

The fact that after careful analysis the aspects to be compared in each legal system remain in some important senses apples and oranges is not bad. The real power of comparative analysis arises precisely from the fact that the

---

[9]Shapiro, *supra* note 2, at vii.

process of comparing "apples" and "oranges" forces the comparatist to develop constructs like "fruit." It forces the comparatist to articulate broader categories to accommodate terms that are at least in some significant way functional equivalents and to search on broader levels for functional similarities and differences. For example, consider pretrial discovery in the United States, which permits non-criminal litigants to search widely even in the hands of the opponents for evidence to support their cases. German civil procedure does not recognize a similar general right of one party to look for evidence in the other party's files and among its witnesses outside of the courtroom, but there are some more limited rights to require divulgence of specific information or documents in court.[10]

One might have thought that in looking for analogues to pretrial discovery, there was no need to consider in-court interrogation since U.S. law also provides for that method of eliciting information from the other party and non-party witnesses, but further reflection leads one to see that discovery is but one method of permitting one side to extract information from the other side or from third party witnesses. In-court examination is, of course, another method, and in looking for functional equivalence, one might even want to consider the question of the degree to which both systems shift the burden of proof (or impose strict liability in tort cases) to account for grossly unequal access by the parties to relevant information. Thus the search for functional equivalence with U.S. civil discovery procedures leads to the broader question of how different legal systems handle the inequality between the parties with respect to access to

---

[10]*See generally* Gerber, *Extraterritorial Discovery and the Conflict of Procedural Systems: Germany and the United States*, 34 AM. J. COMP. L. 745, 757–67 (1986).

information.

5.

The comparative method has the potential to lead to even more interesting analysis by inviting the comparatist to give reasons for the similarities and differences among legal systems or to analyze their significance for the cultures under study.

Comparative study could end with a delineation of relevant similarities and differences. This would satisfy the minimum goal of comparative study, and as the previous sections have indicated, that goal alone requires significant legal analysis if the problems of functional equivalence are investigated thoroughly. However, once one has carefully determined similarities and differences between the legal systems under study, a broader field of inquiry presents itself, one that poses fascinating questions of great general interest. One may ask what the reasons are for the similarities and differences among the legal systems under study. Alternatively, to avoid simplistic notions of causality in human society, one may ask what the significance of the identified similarities and differences is for an understanding of the respective legal systems and the broader cultures of which they are a part. In either case, the point of the inquiry is to pay attention to the connections (or lack of connections) between the specific differences and similarities under study and broader, more systemic contrasts among legal systems, and most particularly, broader contrasts among societies and cultures.

Seeking answers to these questions will cause the comparatist to consider not only global comparison of legal systems, but also similarities and differences in the respective political, economic, and social systems and historical traditions of which they are a part. This is the aspect of comparative law that leads the student beyond law to the rest of the humanities and social sciences, maybe even to the natural sciences. This is where the various "law ands" become relevant: law and history, law and economics, law and society, even law and literature. Political science is an allied field of obvious relevance. Comparative linguistics may offer interesting insights. Even geography influences law in some respects. Since law is but a part of the seamless whole of human culture, there is in principle scarcely any field of study that might not shed some light on the reasons for or significance of similarities and differences among legal systems. Really good comparative writing should be informed by at least some of these allied fields and will be to the extent it seeks to explain why there are given similarities or differences among legal systems or seeks to assess the significance of such similarities or differences.[11]

Of course, I am not claiming that one can obtain this benefit or the one described in the foregoing section solely by undertaking comparative study. A very bright person might take the analysis to a broader level of abstraction or seek the connection between law and society without the prompting of the comparative approach. But I am claiming that the comparative method is a particularly good strategy for trying to secure these intellectual benefits. Under the comparative method, all scholars, not just the especially brilliant, are likely to recognize the necessity of finding broader levels of abstraction and connections between law and society to the extent that the comparison turns up law that remains on

---

[11]In making this statement, I am mindful that chance may also play a significant role in the process by which law is formed or transplanted. *See, e.g.*, Ajani, *By Chance and Prestige: Legal Transplants in Russia and Eastern Europe*, 43 AM. J. COMP. L. 93 (1995). Nevertheless, even that "explanation" cannot be adopted without consideration of other factors relating to the broader cultural contexts of each legal system under comparison.

some significant formal or functional level different in the various legal jurisdictions being studied.

6.

In establishing what the law is in each jurisdiction under study, comparative Law (and, for that matter, studies of foreign law, as well) should (a) be concerned to describe the normal conceptual world of the lawyers, (b) take into consideration all the sources upon which a lawyer in that legal system might base her opinion as to what the law is, and (c) take into consideration the gap between the law on the books and law in action, as well as (d) important gaps in available knowledge about either the law on the books or the law in action.

I have now described the basic method and value of comparing law, but I need to say more about the specific rules for carrying out the comparison. This section lays down guidelines for determining what the law is in each country under comparison. These comments apply equally well, of course, to non-comparative treatments of foreign law.

(a) Focus on the Normal Conceptual World of the Lawyers

I agree with Ewald that the primary task for which comparative lawyers are prepared by their training and experience is to compare law from the interior point of view - that is, to help lawyers from one legal system see how lawyers in another legal system think about certain legal problems.[12] I do not want to lay down narrow definitions of what is and what is not comparative law for fear of choking off interesting work that might not fit my definition. Moreover, comparative law by definition takes one outside of one's own legal tradition and therefore facilitates the taking of an exterior viewpoint of

---

[12]Ewald, *supra* note 2, at 1973–74.

the law. I also have no problem with the kind of political science that treats law as the output of a black box and seeks to explain that output by correlation with other factors exterior to the law, and I have no objection to lawyers contributing to that kind of study as long as they do a good job. Indeed, I think that lawyers should be interested in such studies especially insofar as they shed light on the workings of the legal system and suggest factors at work other than those called out explicitly by legal doctrine. But I do wish to insist that comparative law studies should normally compare the interior views of legal systems, whatever else they may also do. Comparative work therefore usually ought to address the question, "How does the foreign lawyer appear to think about this question and how does that compare to the way we think about it in our legal system?"

This focus on the conceptual world of the lawyer suggests first and foremost a focus on formal legal reasoning. What counts as a source of law in each system under study? Using the law stated in the formal sources of law, what arguments can be made in each system with respect to the legal question under study and how would they be evaluated by well-trained lawyers in each system respectively? In some systems, like that of the United States with its common law heritage and explicitly political ways of selecting judges, lawyers tend to include a consideration of broader questions of policy in their formal legal reasoning and may also take into consideration the political dimensions of a legal problem in analyzing how a court will likely decide a given issue. These kinds of policy considerations and political calculations should also be included as part of the mental world of the well-trained lawyer in such a system. Furthermore, as Ewald has pointed out,[13] appreciating what does and does not count as a good argument in a foreign legal system requires an understanding of the general philosophical traditions of that culture, at least to the extent that they may have influenced the jurists.

(b) Taking Account of All Sources of Information About the Law

The focus on lawyers' argumentation will counteract the tendency to focus on statutory materials only and will force the comparatist to consult cases and the commentary of scholars, as well. In Sacco's terms, the comparatist will have to deal with the variety of "legal formants" - that is, all the authorities a lawyer working in a given system might consult to find the law, from formal sources of law like constitutions and statutes to authorities that are not recognized as formal sources of law but which are nevertheless influential, such as the writings of jurists.[14] The point of Sacco's formulation is that these legal formants may or may not be in harmony. Indeed, on many important questions, there are likely to be in any legal system that has any substantial degree of autonomy from other political institutions a number of conflicting opinions about what the legal rule is. By paying attention to all the relevant legal formants, the comparatist will be saved from taking a more simplistic view of the law than does the foreign legal culture the comparatist is studying.

(c) The Gap Between Law on the Books and Law in Action

The discussion of legal formants shows that one cannot confine one's search for foreign law to the statute books. Other

---

[13] *Id.*

[14] Sacco, *Legal Formants: A Dynamic Approach to Comparative Law,* 39 AM. J. COMP. L. 1 (1991) and 39 AM. J. COMP. L. 343 (1991); see especially 39 AM. J. COMP. L. at 22.

legal formants, such as court opinions or the writings of scholars, may show that what is regarded as the law in that society is quite different from what one might have thought it to be if one looked only at the statutes. There thus may be, and probably are in most legal systems, important gaps between the law in the statute books and the law actually applied by the courts. Comparative law should be interested in both, and especially in the explanations and rationales given by participants in the legal system to explain the gap because these explanations may reveal a great deal about legal reasoning in that system.

There are also in all countries gaps between the law applied by courts and the law under which people live who for some reason - poverty, ignorance, attachment to traditional lifestyles, prejudice, corruption, or fear of political persecution - are unable or unwilling to invoke the protection of the formal legal rule. Because lawyers are interested not just in formal legal argumentation, but also in the actual impact of law in the world, the comparatist should be interested in this gap, as well. Perceptions of the gap may influence legal reasoning. In Brazil, for example, the gap between the law on the books and law in action has been so evident to Brazilians that it has a special name, the jeito, and it has, at least in some forms, become a highly prized legal or social institution for obtaining fairness amid the chaos of the formal legal system.[15] It may be especially easy to see this kind of gap in foreign legal systems, but the comparatist should also be on the lookout for it in his own legal system because no legal system is entirely immune to this phenomenon.

Finally, there are also in all countries situations in which the impact of a particular legal rule is affected by

---

[15]Rosenn, *Brazil's Legal Culture: The Jeito Revisited*, 1 FLA. INT'L L.J. 1 (1984).

practices which are not part of the formal law. For example, the effect that the consideration doctrine could have to hinder the commercial use of options in U.S. law is greatly mitigated by the practice of granting them in return for nominal payment. Medieval Islamic law even developed a rich literature on the subject of legal devices which were forthrightly intended to permit parties to circumvent certain legal proscriptions, like that against payment of interest.[16] In trying to assess the functional equivalence of two systems of rules, it is important to have information about contracting and other practices which may either attenuate or magnify the impact of the rules.

(d) Gaps in Information About Foreign Law

Those who study U.S. law in the large research libraries in the United States become accustomed to having a great deal of information available about their subject, from complete collections of statutes and regulations to extensive case reports, a burgeoning "how-to" literature for the actual practice, and an extensive academic literature. There is even a growing literature about empirical studies of the real-world effects of many aspects of law in the United States. But comparative law studies are dogged by enormous gaps in the information available. First, libraries' collections of foreign law are hardly ever as complete as the best libraries in the foreign country itself. Second, countries of the civil law tradition do not publish the decisions of appellate courts with the thoroughness and persistence of common law countries. Third, despite the growth of fields like legal sociology, it is often difficult to find empirical studies of the aspects of U.S. law in which a scholar is interested; it is even more difficult to

---

[16]ABRAHAM L. UDOVITCH, PARTNERSHIP AND PROFIT IN MEDIEVAL ISLAM 11–12 (1970).

find relevant empirical studies for many other countries, especially third-world countries.

Good comparative writing should show concern for this issue and should deal honestly and forthrightly with it. The reader should bear this concern in mind in evaluating comparative and foreign law studies. Has the author cited the most recent sources for what is represented to be current law? Are there reasons to believe that the sources available to the author are not current? Has the author cited such a reasonable assortment of commentators or such distinguished commentators that the views represented to be the dominant views in a given legal system are not likely to be the idiosyncratic views of one person or group? Has the author presented any information about law in action so that the reader can see whether or not there is a gap between it and the law on the books? If so, does the author cite reliable sources for that information? (Anecdotal evidence is not necessarily objectionable. Much comparative law is based on anecdotal evidence of law in action. It is not, however, systematic and hence may not accurately represent the norm, and careful comparative analysis should recognize this limitation.)

In short, good comparatists should be sensitive to the ever present limitations on information available about foreign legal systems and should qualify their conclusions if they are unable to have access to sufficient information or if they have reason to suspect that they are missing important information. If the gaps are too large, the study should not be undertaken at all because its conclusions about foreign law will be too uncertain to be useful.

7.

Comparative and foreign law scholarship both require strong linguistic skills and maybe even the skills of anthropological field study in order to collect information about foreign legal systems at first hand, but it is also reasonable for the comparative scholar without the necessary linguistic skill or in-country experience to rely on secondary literature in languages the comparatist can read, subject to the usual caution about using secondary literature.

How does a comparatist gain enough information about a foreign legal system to engage in comparison? Reading a foreign statute written in a language other than the comparatist's native language takes considerable linguistic skill, and going beyond statutes to consult the wide variety of potentially relevant legal formants takes an even greater degree of fluency because of the volume of literature to be read. Thus scholars of foreign law, whether or not they are also doing explicit comparison, obviously need to be fluent in at least one main language of each of the foreign countries whose law they intend to study. In-depth knowledge of the history of the country and its peoples and its philosophical and religious traditions is necessary to understand the indigenous forms of legal reasoning and value judgments. In addition, in-country experience is obviously useful to ensure that the foreign scholar adequately appreciates the cultural and geographical context for the foreign legal system. Moreover, actual legal study and research in the foreign country or at least considerable contact with lawyers or law professors from that country is very helpful to ensure that the foreign legal scholar is correctly understanding the general pattern of legal reasoning in the foreign country.

Finally, in-country experience is crucial for learning about the actual practices and social conditions that may create gaps between the law on the books and law in action. To the extent these are documented in the foreign country's literature, it would not of course be necessary for the foreign law scholar to gather information about them, but they often are not. It would thus be desirable for foreign law scholars to supplement their linguistic skills with the field observation skills of an anthropologist. Most comparatists and foreign law scholars, like me, are not so trained, but many of us have enjoyed substantial in-country exposure to one or more of the systems on which we write and have not hesitated to document our anecdotal observations about the workings of the foreign systems. As indicated above, this unsystematic information is probably better than no information at all, but has to be evaluated with caution.

Pure foreign law scholarship and the foreign law portion of comparative law scholarship thus ideally involve formidable linguistic knowledge (at least where the foreign law is in a foreign language) and substantial historical and cultural knowledge, as well as actual experience in the country and in contact with its lawyers. Such scholarship would even be enhanced by training in anthropological field methods. These demands call for a huge scholarly investment. To the beginner, especially the student, it may seem virtually impossible to gain the required base of knowledge and experience.

There are two points I wish to make about the knowledge and experience needed to gain a proper understanding of foreign law. First, the burden involved in obtaining it is a good reason why some scholars choose to specialize in foreign law and minimize explicit comparison. While I wish to encourage broader use of explicit comparison, I recognize that comparison requires considerable knowledge of at least a second legal system. Acquiring that knowledge may conflict with acquiring the in-depth knowledge of the first legal system. No one can amass that kind of knowledge about every part of the globe, and in order to keep scholars without the full grounding necessary to be an expert in a particular country's law from serious error, there is a need for some country specialists to devote most of their energies to specialized study of a given country or group of countries, especially in the case of cultural traditions radically different from those of the scholar's own country and especially if the main language is very different from the scholar's native tongue. Specialization and team efforts comprise a better solution than asking every scholar to spread himself too thin. The foreign law specialist and the comparatist stand in symbiotic relationship. I would, however, suggest that since most foreign law scholars have considerable knowledge of their own domestic system, most foreign law scholars could include explicit comparison with the scholar's own system without detracting much from the pursuit of knowledge about the foreign legal system.

Second, it is quite legitimate for comparatists to base their comparisons on literature produced by foreign law specialists, at least to a substantial degree. The comparatist need not have first-hand knowledge of all the foreign law upon which he bases his comparisons, but she needs to be a discriminating consumer of the available scholarly writing, whether it is explicitly comparative or not. The comparatist should evaluate secondary literature on foreign law in accordance with the foregoing observations about what is required. Does the author possess the necessary linguistic knowledge? Do his citations show that he has canvassed adequately the various legal formants? Has she made good use of translations of important, relevant legal literature from the foreign country if there are any? Has he reported on actual practices in the country based on his own experiences or on reliable reports by others? Do the author's comments appear to be informed by a deep understanding of the nation's cultural and religious traditions and history? It may be difficult for the non-foreign-law-specialist to make these judgments with any confidence. As in all types of research beyond personal knowledge, healthy skepticism, a search for corroboration from multiple sources, and attention to academic reputation should help.

8.
Comparative law scholarship should be organized in a way that emphasizes explicit comparison.

Finally I come to the nitty-gritty detail of organization. I do not wish to dictate matters of form narrowly. Good writers find the organization that best fits their subject. However, I want to encourage the use of organization for comparative writing that emphasizes the comparative task being accomplished. There are all too many examples of comparative books and articles in which the comparative exploration of a subject (antitrust, for example) is organized in the following way: a detailed description of the antitrust law of country A, followed by a detailed description of the antitrust law of country B, followed by a brief section that attempts to draw the chief comparisons. But this last section is inevitably too short and too lacking in detail to be effective comparison, not only because the writer has run out of steam at the end of the work, but also because, if he were to support his comparative analysis with all the rich detail, he would have to repeat much of the first two sections. It is as if the writer said to the reader, "Here is all the raw data about this subject in the two legal systems I am studying. Now you do the comparison according to these general guidelines I am giving you!"

Instead of the simplistic, ineffective, and inefficient three-part approach, I advocate trying as much as possible to make every section comparative. For example, if the subject is antitrust law, one section might compare and contrast the development of antitrust law in each country, another the two countries' treatment of horizontal restraints of trade, another the vertical restraints, another the enforcement mechanisms and remedies, etc. Try to break the subject down into the natural units that are important to the analysis and then describe each country's law with respect to that unit and compare and contrast them immediately. Let the contrasts documented in each section build toward your overall conclusion.[17]   Of course, for certain subjects it may be necessary to describe the law of one country in a block before comparing it. This seems especially likely, for example, when what is being compared is the historical development of a field or legal system.[18]   But the shorter these blocks, the more effective will be the comparison.

9.

Comparative studies should be undertaken in a spirit of respect for the other.

The last point concerns the attitude a comparatist should have. So much in foreign legal systems seems so bizarre that it shocks us. Why do the Germans and French disdain the U.S. practice of intrusive party-led discovery in civil cases? To the U.S. lawyer, it almost seems as if the Germans and French must not be that interested in finding the truth. To the German and French lawyers, it seems as if the U.S. system fails to protect individual privacy. Neither system is contemptible simply because it is different from the other. In analyzing a foreign legal system, the comparative scholar has to make extraordinary efforts to discern the sense of foreign rules and arrangements.

---

[17]For one successful example of this type of organization on a large scale, see INTERNATIONAL ENCYCLOPEDIA OF COMPARATIVE LAW, VOL. XI, TORTS (Andre Tunc ed., 1983).

[18]*See, e.g.*, JOHN P. DAWSON, THE ORACLES OF THE LAW (1968).

I want to emphasize that I mean by this to suggest a working method only, not a limit on what comparative scholars may say. I have already said in Section 3 above that comparative law may be undertaken for any purpose, including a critical one. Indeed, constructive criticism is a sincere form of respect. Moreover, at the end of the day, criticism should be judged, not by the critic's attitude, but by the reasonableness of her premises and the force of her logic. However, before the comparatist criticizes, she must make all possible efforts to avoid a narrowly chauvinistic view. She must try to see the sense of the foreign arrangements even if they are strangely different from her own and seem to represent values directly contrary to her own.

The comparatist must also bear in mind that criticism coming from an outsider is always suspect on the grounds of chauvinism. This is all the more reason to be cautious in criticizing foreign law, but it is much less of a problem when the same piece of scholarship levels the same or a similar criticism against the author's own legal system. Criticism of a foreign legal system is also less likely to be dismissed as chauvinistic if it is supported by citation to domestic critics of the system. Nevertheless, sometimes a foreign legal system's disregard for certain values compels one to criticize even in the absence of support from the target legal system, especially in situations involving authoritarian governments, in which only the foreigners may have the possibility of publishing their criticism. God grant us the wisdom to know when to speak out forcefully!

***

Summary

The foregoing nine principles comprise, I believe, the basic elements of the comparative method for studying law. The method is not complicated. In fact, it is so simple that I

51

for long have hesitated to dignify it with the term "method." I have come to realize, however, that while the comparative method is simple to describe, it is difficult to apply because satisfactory results can be obtained only if the one making the comparisons has command of a large amount of information about the legal systems under comparison, as well as the broader societies in which the legal systems exist. This factor may explain at least some of the general disappointment with comparative law: It is difficult to do well. Nevertheless, it is ever more indispensable in our interconnected and shrinking world. It offers at least two significant intellectual benefits that are not easily obtained outside of the comparative method: (1) the tendency to push analytic categories to higher levels of abstraction in order to bridge differences between legal systems, and (2) the tendency to force the researcher to expand the analysis to include the whole legal system and its relationship with the rest of human culture and its material and spiritual context in order to understand the differences and similarities observed. For these reasons, comparative law truly holds exciting potential to help us better understand law and legal systems.

III. GUIDE FOR THE LEGAL WRITING PROCESS

1. Seminar Papers in General

According to Prof. Eugene Volokh, successful seminar papers possess several common characteristics.[1] Depending on the requirements of your professor, your paper should seek to achieve these same things.[2] First, the student should strive to write on a topic that will not result in an obvious answer. A quality paper, structured on a nonobvious topic, is contrasted with a paper that makes a self-evident, undisputed observation on an issue of law or that makes only the slightest of changes to existing scholarship. Papers that apply settled law to marginally new fact patterns will rarely achieve nonobviousness.

In addition to writing on a nonobvious topic, the student should also ensure that the arguments presented in the paper are based on sound reasoning. In other words, both the arguments that you make and the paper itself should be sound, reasonable, and sensible. While your piece should, in order to retain the reader's attention, be interesting and perhaps even bold, it should also avoid making outlandish, unjustifiable claims.

Beyond the technical requirements of nonobviousness and soundness, you should also make sure that the paper itself is written in an interesting style. Your professor really

---

[1] Adapted from EUGENE VOLOKH, ACADEMIC LEGAL WRITING: LAW REVIEW ARTICLES, STUDENT NOTES, SEMINAR PAPERS, AND GETTING ON LAW REVIEW 9–34 (3d ed. 2007).

[2] Similarly, commentators Fajans and Falk assert that successful papers are "original, . . . comprehensive[,] . . . meticulously correct, . . . [and both] clear and readable." *See* ELIZABETH FAJANS & MARY R. FALK, SCHOLARLY WRITING FOR LAW STUDENTS: SEMINAR PAPERS, LAW REVIEW NOTES AND LAW REVIEW COMPETITION PAPERS 4–5 (3d ed. 2005).

has no choice about whether to read your paper. This fact does not, however, warrant failing to attempt to write an interesting paper. In addition to being an exercise in formulating and discussing original ideas in a certain legal field, the seminar paper is also a way to teach you how to write better.

Another characteristic of a quality seminar paper is one that provides excellent, well-structured background information on the subject. The structure of this section may vary depending on your professor's requirements. Your professor may be willing to accept that you understand the background of a subject and thus not require you to include such sections in your paper. Others, however, will require you to write about the background to help you learn to write these sections. Moreover, because seminar papers are often used as the basis for subsequent law journal articles, students should keep in mind that future readers, especially young practitioners and those new to a particular area of law, will find a concise historical background to be quite useful.

The student should also focus on writing seminar papers that address practical issues that the author or others who are similarly situated may face in their daily practice. In other words, depending on the requirements of your professor or your own goals, your paper and its topic should be grounded in reality. While there is something to be said for abstraction and purely academic pursuits, your paper should have an impact on, and be useful to, actual practitioners in the legal area on which you are writing. Because your seminar paper is only being written for one reader (i.e., your professor), you may be able to relax this requirement. On the other hand, remember that seminar papers often serve as the basis for future articles; therefore, a practical or practice-based seminar paper may prove quite useful well beyond the seminar on which it was based.

Finally, quality papers provide innovative solutions. Depending on the requirements of your professor or your own goals, your paper should achieve some level of novelty; it should make an original claim. This requires creative thinking and originality. Do not, however, make the mistake of manufacturing a problem or inventing an inconsistency. Truth should not be sacrificed for originality.

Achieving novelty serves several purposes in the seminar paper setting. First, your class is probably geared to helping you think creatively. If your paper addresses an emerging issue or provides a fresh perspective, it shows your professor that you were able to get important information out of the class. Second, originality is always more difficult than rehashing the ideas of others. If your paper shows novelty, it proves to your professor that you put in the work necessary to come up with an original idea. Third, it makes a good impression on your professor.

2. Topic Selection and Research

Although the idea of selecting a seminar paper topic may seem daunting at first, there are several sources from which you may draw during the selection process.[3] First, remember that your professor, as an expert in the field that your class discusses, will have a very good idea of what issues are contentious. Accordingly, he can recommend good seminar paper topics. While some professors may be hesitant to recommend ideas, it doesn't hurt to ask.

Often, class discussions will highlight areas of a particular field that have yet to be settled or that, while

---

[3]For an informative article on topic selection, see Heather Meeker, *Stalking the Golden Topic: A Guide to Locating and Selecting Topics for Legal Research Papers*, 1996 UTAH L. REV. 917 (1996).

settled, are on tenuous grounds. You can identify such issues and problems by noting a lack of consensus during the class discussions. If you think you've identified an unsettled issue in the class discussions, be sure to get your professor's thoughts. There is a possibility that you will, consciously or subconsciously, use ideas expressed by your classmates during the discussion. This shouldn't be a problem because your analysis will be much more in depth than the class discussion.

Similarly, scholarly articles will implicitly leave certain issues unanswered or explicitly acknowledge that an answer has yet to arise. Recognizing these situations will help you decide on a topic that will lend itself to novelty. You probably shouldn't write your paper as a response to an article. Instead, write about the issue which the article raises.

Keeping abreast of current events is another way to find a topic that will lead to a novel, interesting paper. You can write on a specific event and what bearing it has on a certain legal institution or process. Alternatively, you can identify a more general problem with the legal process which may be the source of some newsworthy event. Be sure to consult a plethora of sources, such as television, internet, magazines, and leading newspapers such as the *New York Times*[4] or the *Washington Post*.

Finally, you may receive inspiration for your topic from standard legal databases, as well as weblogs ("blogs") that are hosted by respected legal practitioners and scholars. Both LexisNexis and Westlaw feature searchable databases for articles in all major news publications, as well as jurisdiction- and area-specific resources that highlight emerging

---

[4]For example, Fajans and Falk comment that "On just one day during the writing of this chapter, *The New York Times* contained some twenty stories that raised legal issues." FAJANS AND FALK, *supra* note 2, at 19.

developments in the law. In addition to these databases, many practitioners and scholars maintain their own blogs, on which they discuss emerging legal issues. When using internet blogs, however, be sure to verify the reputation of the site owner as well as the accuracy of the information discussed.

After you have found your topic, it is important that you identify which issues within that topic are contentious, unsettled, misunderstood, or generally of interest. You can find these issues by researching cases, journal articles, or the news. Depending on how you decided on a topic to discuss, you might already be well on your way to identifying the important issues. Moreover, you will also need to find other cases, incidents, and articles that bear on your topic.[5] This can be done by:

- Reading the cases that cite one of your important cases.
- Reading the cases to which one or several of your cases cites.
- Search for cases and articles that use keywords that may be unique to your topic. While there may be several cases and articles that obliquely reference your topic, you can eliminate many of these by using Westlaw and Lexis features that narrow your search. Examples of features that limit your search focus are the "synopsis" and "summary" functions on Westlaw and the "summary" and "syllabus" functions on Lexis.
- Search for administrative agency decisions and attorney general opinions.
- Research the news and history of the events that led to your issue.
- Research any legislative history that might relate to your issue.
- Do a general internet search on your issue. This probably won't result in useable sources, but with search engines like Google and the growing popularity

[5]Fajans and Falk suggest keeping a reading journal during this stage. *See* FAJANS & FALK, *supra* note 2, at 37–39.

of Wikipedia, you can find a lot of information that will broaden your research ideas.

It is essential that you fully understand the system of laws and regulations governing the issue your paper will discuss. A failure to achieve this understanding will be evident immediately to any learned reader. The easiest way to understand the framework is to start with the broadest possible overview of your issue and work your way down to the minutiae. There are many materials available to provide this broad overview. For example, commercial exam preparation outlines and West's *Nutshell* series are good places to start. In general, these sources are concise, informative, and easy to understand.

After gaining some level of proficiency with your general topic, find a treatise. Bear in mind one of the most important maxims of treatise research: not all treatises are created equal and not all treatises are based on the same ideology. Asking a professor which treatise or treatises are most respected in a field will help you find the right ones. While reading the treatise, pay close attention to the footnotes. These will broaden the scope of your research so that you don't miss any nuances in the field you are researching. After understanding the treatise (or those important chapters for your purposes), reread the cases and statutory provisions you found to identify those that are most relevant.

Once you have researched the broad issues with the treatise, you should next consult legal periodicals such as law reviews, specialty journals, and bar journals. These will help you understand and identify new developments in your field of study as well as recognize the direction in which experts are heading. Additionally, there may be cases that, in order to be taken seriously by most scholars, you must discuss in your paper. These cases will usually come to your attention in your treatise and periodical research, but an independent search of cases dealing with your issue might also be helpful.

Before you begin to collect your research materials, be sure to have a predetermined method for organizing your sources.[6] Also, it is wise to print off all of the most important materials that you will use (e.g., cases, statutes, articles) so that you may refer to it frequently.[7] Finally, it is critical to determine whether there are any forthcoming articles on your topic. The Social Science Research Network database is one of the best sources for this research.

3. Writing

Once you have identified the goals of your paper and have conducted the necessary preliminary research, it is time to begin writing.[8] A few useful instructions at this stage will help students to eliminate frustration, overcome stress and anxiety, and enjoy the writing process.

First, establish a permanent writing schedule and follow it religiously. Begin by looking for time slots in your schedule that leave you completely free to focus on the task at hand. Do not accept or make phone calls, read emails, surf the internet, or allow any other distractions during this period. If you find yourself distracted at home or school, find an alternate location that will allow you to concentrate. Following a permanent writing schedule produces several benefits. First, you will find yourself more productive and more focused. Second, it allows you to budget your time, discourages you from allow the project to take over your other activities and responsibilities, and reduces stress. Finally, this approach

---

[6]Marie-Pierre Granger, *Researching and Writing Tips* (May 19, 2003) (on file with author).
[7]*Id.*
[8]*See generally* VOLOKH, *supra* note 1, at 102–33.

ensures that you do not leave writing projects until the last minute, which will most likely result in a higher quality product.

Next, there is simply no better advice than this: start writing now. Do not procrastinate, no matter how overwhelmed you may feel by the size of the project. Furthermore, if you start the writing process early enough, there will be plenty of time to write more drafts. It is easy to get into the habit of trying to make every draft your last draft; similarly, it is easy to try to write every section and paragraph like it's the last time you'll have to write it. Instead, write the first draft quickly and finish it in only a few sittings.[9] You can do this by, when getting stuck, moving on to a new section without hesitation. If you suddenly have an idea to a section you've moved past, go back and get it down on paper. This will ensure that you get all your ideas out in this first draft. Another benefit to finishing your first draft quickly is that it allows you enough time for the topic to mature in your mind.[10] You can use this additional time to discuss the topic with professors, to gain feedback from your colleagues, and to supplement your topic with additional sources.[11]

Finishing the first draft in a timely manner will require planning on your part. As part of your writing schedule, set reasonable writing goals for each day and give yourself mini-deadlines to finish sections or chapters.[12] In your planning, be sure to include extra time to account for unexpected events, such as computer problems, illness, and so forth.[13] Although

---

[9]Other commentators refer to this as a "dump" or "zero" draft. *See, e.g.*, FAJANS & FALK, *supra* note 2, at 59–63.

[10]*Granger, supra* note 6.

[11]*Granger, supra* note 6.

[12]*Granger, supra* note 6.

[13]*Granger, supra* note 3. It is also advisable to backup your document on a daily basis, preferably onto a variety of media in different locations to ensure that you have a number of recovery

it will be a messy draft, getting it done early means that you can go back and write several more drafts with plenty of time to spare. Finishing a rough draft early enough to have time to go through several more drafts is easier said than done. This process is crucial to good writing. Going through five, ten, or even fifteen drafts should be your goal. The trick is to start early and get all your ideas on paper as soon as possible, no matter how sloppy or imprecise they are. The sooner you do this, the sooner you can refine your ideas.

As you are going through the process of improving your drafts, try to put yourself in the shoes of your most critical reader. Identify the slightest points of contention and ask yourself: *what is the counter-argument?* The difficulty here is that his process may lead you to believe that the argument in opposition to your own is the more reasonable, logical one. While changing your position will necessarily lead to more drafts, finding the most defendable position should certainly be worth the extra work. Do not be afraid if your initial drafts do not proceed in a logical fashion. This is just a function of getting your ideas on paper as soon as possible. Good organization can come later. Starting quickly, regardless of bad organization, is a sure-fire way to avoid writer's block and make sure you address all of the key issues.

Once you have written several drafts and have identified (and hopefully addressed) the counterarguments, it is vital to take a step back and view the work as a whole.

Read through your paper as if you have never read it before. If you get to a sentence or a paragraph that you have

---

options in case of data loss. Many students store copies of the draft onto CD-ROMs or USB jump drives. Also, students often send backup files to an email address that is accessible from any internet browser. This technique is especially useful for free email accounts like Gmail that offer archival technology to their users. *See generally* http//mail.google.com (last visited Apr. 5, 2008).

to re-read, there is a very good chance your reader will have to re-read it. Whether the problem is one of poor organization or simple awkwardness, it must be rewritten because your job is to make your paper as readable and understandable as possible. Only then will your reader understand your issue, which is really your ultimate goal.

When revising your draft, be sure not to stray too far to the opposite end of the spectrum—needlessly complex writing. In almost all instances, your audience is composed of highly intelligent people. Your goal should be to get your point across as briefly, simply, and effectively as possible without sacrificing important details or nuances. While writing, you should subject your paper to the utmost scrutiny by asking whether you could convey your argument with fewer, simpler words. Indeed, the sophisticated writer has the ability to clarify even the most complex issues; the inexperienced writer, however, uses verbose sentences in an attempt to impress the reader with his vocabulary.

After numerous drafts, most authors will discover that it becomes quite difficult to gain perspective or identify flaws on their own. This is not an admission of weakness or a sign of inadequacy; rather, it signifies a close connection to the material and is an organic part of the writing process. Therefore, after you have gone through several drafts and edits on your own, it is important to find a knowledgeable reader who can offer un-biased advice. This may be a classmate, associate, or, even better, your professor. This hinges on whether your professor is willing to read an unfinished paper; if your professor is agreeable, you should certainly take advantage of the opportunity. The earlier you get outside editing help, the earlier you can implement any suggestions; be willing to do this as soon as possible. Any suggestions that your reader does have should be applied to the entire paper, not just the section, paragraph, or sentence where the suggestion was given.

Apart from the substantive concerns of a seminar paper, students should also address the structure and organization of the paper.[14] Indeed, the organization of a paper may be a critical component in the readers' ability to understand key concepts, appreciate your arguments, and understand the underlying policies that you advance. First, headings are a great way to keep your reader aware of your general plan. Put simply, understanding the organization of the paper is important to understanding the paper itself. The headings, therefore, should refer to the argument or observation you make in the section or subsection. On the other hand, generic headings are less helpful to the reader. Beyond the impact on the target audience, headings are also useful to the author in organizing his thoughts. Seeing the headings in your own paper will help you quickly identify organizational errors. By following headings, the author may, for example, be able to identify an inadvertent shift between issues that has occurred without a clear distinction. Such shifts confuse the reader and should be avoided.

Closely related to the use of headings is the implementation of a table of contents. The table allows you to observe your overall organization, as reflected by the section and subsection headings, in one easy-to-access place. It also is helpful for readers who wish to review your writing on one narrow issue among the many issues you have addressed in your paper. Otherwise, the reader may have to sift through countless pages of material that is irrelevant for his purposes. A common student error in the use of headings and tables of

---

[14]MARTHA FAULK & IRVING MEHLER, THE ELEMENTS OF LEGAL WRITING: A GUIDE TO THE PRINCIPLES OF WRITING CLEAR, CONCISE, AND PERSUASIVE LEGAL DOCUMENTS 93–99 (1994).

content is consistency. When reviewing your draft after adding headings and a table of contents, ask yourself the following questions. *Is capitalization consistent? Do you use sentence fragments as opposed to whole sentences? Are they grammatically parallel?*

In addition to organizing the material that you already have, you need to have a plan in place to handle new information and set new goals during the writing project. First, new and interesting ideas may strike as you write and it is important to note them before you forget them. The key to handling new information and ideas is to be consistent with the method that you use to process them. One place to do this is below the heading of the section in which these new ideas would appear. Another idea is to keep a writing journal during the project, in which you identify new areas to research, jot down thoughts as they come to you, or list the areas that you plan to address in future drafts. If you implement the journal method, be sure to fill out the journal at the end of each writing session. This preserves your train of thought and prevents the omission of important ideas.

During the writing process, students must be aware of the pitfalls common to academic writing, both in writing and in logic. These may occur despite the best research, planning, and preparation. By keeping these pitfalls in mind as you are writing, you are much less likely to include them in your draft.

There are several common errors in student legal writing.[15] One of the first and foremost errors is the failure to

---

[15]In addition to these common pitfalls, students should also pay careful attention to style, grammar, sentence structure, and other critical aspects of legal writing. For excellent sources on this matter, consult FAULK & MEHLER, *supra* note 14; TERRI LECLERCQ, GUIDE TO LEGAL WRITING STYLE (4th ed. 2007); HOWARD DARMSTADTER, HEREOF, THEREOF, AND EVERYWHEREOF: A CONTRARIAN GUIDE TO LEGAL WRITING (2002); WILLIAM STRUNK, JR. & E.B. WHITE, THE ELEMENTS OF STYLE (4th ed. 2000); RICHARD C. WYDICK, PLAIN ENGLISH FOR LAWYERS

use topic sentences. Topic sentences guide the reader through the paragraph and give an idea of what is to come. The lack of topic sentences forces the reader to identifying your main points for you. This is lazy writing and often results in misunderstanding and misinterpretation. Similarly, ensure that each paragraph introduces, discuss, and conclude a single idea. Adhering to this approach will create disciplined writing and will help your reader more clearly understand your argument.

In terms of paragraph structures, students must strive for concise, digestible paragraphs. Long paragraphs make the reader's job of deciphering your argument more difficult. If a paragraph is so long that it contains two, three, or four distinct ideas, the reader will find it difficult to distinguish them. This can leave holes in the reader's understanding of your general argument, making it less likely that he or she will adopt your solution.

Moreover, your reader should clearly understand why one paragraph comes after another. The use of transitional words and phrases, therefore, is paramount. When transitioning between paragraphs, be sure to ask yourself some basic questions. *Is the next paragraph simply providing another illustration of the concept in the previous? Is the next paragraph providing the counter-argument to the previous? Is the next paragraph analogizing to another rule, law, or case? Does the next paragraph illustrate a solution different from the one shown in the previous?* The type of transitional phrase that you use will change depending on the relation between the paragraphs, whether you are comparing, contrasting, analogizing, and so forth.

(4th ed. 1998); THE ELEMENTS OF LEGAL WRITING: A GUIDE TO THE PRINCIPLES OF WRITING CLEAR, CONCISE, AND PERSUASIVE LEGAL DOCUMENTS (1994).

Another common error in student writing is the failure to write with assertive, active language. This is often seen when students reiterate the same point several times during the course of a paper. If you find the desire to repeat yourself, ask whether you said it clearly and assertively the first time. If so, rewrite the material in its first instance. Similarly, avoid the excessive use of introductory phrases such as "it is important to note," "it should be noted," and so forth. Students use such phrases because they believe it will focus the reader's attention. Instead, it simply becomes clutter on the page. Furthermore, such phrases are largely irrelevant: if the material is in the text, it is presumed that it is something that is important to remember or consider. Finally, be sure to always use the active voice. Because passive voice is less direct than active voice, it requires more words. This makes reading the sentence more difficult and time-consuming. Identifying the actor is a critical element in legal writing because it may determine, *inter alia*, who bears a legal duty, who is liable for particular conduct, who bears a particular burden of proof or persuasion, and so forth. Passive sentences, therefore, are inappropriate in legal writing because they often omit the actor altogether.

In addition to writing errors, students should be mindful to avoid logical pitfalls as well. Indeed, the most persuasive argument will lose its impact if it contains even minor errors in logic. Fortunately, these pitfalls are largely avoidable with enough care and attention.

First, it is critical to define any terms that are not universally understood before constructing your arguments. The use of undefined terms results in sloppy writing and leaves the reader questioning what you mean. Many ordinary, commonplace words—"reasonableness" is a good example— are also legal terms of art and have entirely different meanings in a legal context. You should explain precisely what you are intending to convey when you use these words and others that invite uncertainty.

Once you have defined the terms you will be using, avoid extremes in language when constructing your argument. As a law student, how often have you encountered a rule of law that has no exception whatsoever? Rarely, if ever. Thus, phrases such as "never," always," or "impossible" should be avoided. More than likely, it is possible to see exceptions to the rule you propose or the position that you advance. Generalizations leave the impression that the author is more concerned with being "right" than with finding a solution.

Similarly, students should avoid arguing for the adoption of an "either/or" rule. Rarely is there only one alternative to a given approach. Announcing that the correct approach can be only X or Y misleads the reader into thinking that the debate is limited to those alternatives and, in turn, undercuts your thesis. While you may not even be aware of all the potential alternatives, you should acknowledge that they might exist.

In arguing for the adoption of a new rule or approach, be sure to avoid the use of extreme arguments simply to advance your theory. For example, you should not imply that a law is wrong because it is imperfect. Because most legislatures and courts favor a flexible approach to solving legal problems, by its very nature it is impossible for a single rule of law to address every possible scenario. Arguing that the law is bad because of such a shortcoming is a weak criticism. Instead, argue that the formulation which your paper endorses will address more scenarios than the current regime.

Similarly, it is equally ineffective to use a "slippery slope" argument without careful consideration. Almost any piece of legislation that is enforced without discretion or limits could lead to oppression. In other words, stating that one law or another puts us on a "slippery slope" produces nothing novel and adds nothing to the debate. Rather than making this assertion, identify competing legal regimes and argue why one is more likely to have negative consequences.

Finally, the use of metaphors, though powerful, can hide logical errors. For example, use of the "chilled speech" metaphor[16] implies that the law in question will deter speech in an unconstitutional manner. By relying solely on the metaphor, the student fails to show how the speech might be deterred. Therefore, in plain terms state the effect you think the law will have and, then, defend your assertion.

---

[16] VOLOKH, *supra* note 1, at 134.

IV. RESEARCH AND PROOF OF TRANSNATIONAL LAW

1. Proper Use of Evidence

Improper use of authorities can result in embarrassment, ridicule, and, worst of all, the loss of your colleagues' respect.[1] One of the easiest ways to fall into the trap of misusing authority is to fail to use the original source. If you want to quote a proposition stated by a particular court in a particular case, you need to read, quote, and cite that source. Do not borrow the quote you want to use from a law review article or another case.

The preference for primary source materials exists for several reasons. First, there is the possibility that the secondary source has misquoted the proposition you want to use. This misquotation could range from the omission of an unimportant "the" or "a" to the very important substation of "inconsequential" with "consequential." Do not let one individual's mistake become your mistake. Second, there could also be contextual problems. For example, a court may make a statement that, taken out of context, would not have the same meaning as the court intended. This change in context may be intentional or unintentional. But if you use a quotation from a secondary source without reading the primary source from which the quotation was taken, you risk the possibility of using the quotation out of context. This is unfair to the author you are quoting as well as the reader who will be misled.

---

[1] Adapted from VOLOKH, *supra* note 1, at 134–43.

2. Comparative Law Research

RUDOLPH B. SCHLESINGER ET AL., COMPARTIVE LAW: CASES AND MATERIALS 999–1004 (6th ed. 1998)[*]

a.   A Brief Introduction to Comparative Law Research

Research in foreign legal systems is often subject to substantial difficulties due to the non-availability of materials. In addition, the inexperienced researcher may go astray even in the face of plentiful sources.   No comparative research should be undertaken without an awareness of the special pitfalls and hazards implicit in such research. The preceding chapter of this book on the Special Hazards of Comparative Law is an introduction to these problems. This Appendix has the more modest purpose of giving some initial hints as to sources. The last few years have seen a great expansion of electronic source materials; these will be covered first before dealing with more traditional items. The researcher should be aware, however, that before focusing the research on specific issues (for which electronic sources are often excellent), the researcher will need some knowledge of the basic structures, concepts and principles underlying the legal systems which are to be the focus of the project.   The printed word is generally still the best source for that endeavor. A number of relevant materials will be mentioned in part B of this Appendix.

---

[*]Reprinted with permission from Foundation Press

i. Electronic Sources
a. The Internet

In spite of the recent enthusiasm for the Internet, it is probably less useful for detailed research than might be expected. The commercial providers of legal source material in the United States, chiefly Lexis-Nexis and Westlaw, also operate to some extent in foreign countries, or have their local counterparts (such as Juris in France, where Lexis, however, is also active). Understandably, data bases available through commercial providers are not accessible over the Internet, or accessible only with a password requiring a prior subscription.

There are, however, a number of items that may be of interest to the researcher. A selection is listed here. No attempt, however, is made to provide a complete list, since the relevant entries change so rapidly.

The Office of the Assistant Legal Adviser for Private International Law at the Department of State has made a data base available, which includes Convention texts, draft texts, reports, announcements, etc., from UNCITRAL, the Hague Conference on Private International Law, the Rome Institute for the Unification of Private Law (UNIDROIT) and the Organization of American States. The address is http://www.his.com/pildb/.

There are several bases relating to the Vienna Sales Convention. They include one maintained by the United Nations Commission on International Trade Law (UNCITRAL), which also contains materials related to other UNCITRAL work products, such as the UNCITRAL Model Arbitration Law. The data base consists of abstracts of cases relating to these items. The address is: http://www.un.or.at/uncitral/index.html. Information on the Vienna Sales Convention is also available through the University of Pittsburgh Journal of Law and Commerce web site: http://www.pitt.law.edu/journal/welcome/htm.

The Cornell Legal Information Institute (http://www.law.cornell.edu) has, in addition to American legal materials, a file of contemporary constitutions and provides a link with some foreign data bases.

A basic link to various European Community data bases is http://europa.eu.int. (The European Community Delegation in Washington publishes, from time to time, a list of data bases useful for European Community research.)

A number of additional resources are mentioned in D.A. Levy, Internet Resources for Private International Law, American Society of International Law Private International Law Interest Group Newsletter, July 1996, at 1-4.

b.   Commercial services

The two commercial services, Lexis-Nexis and Westlaw, furnish extensive access to data bases containing materials on international, European community, and foreign law. A current list of available materials from these services should be consulted for up-to-date information. Not surprisingly, materials in the English language predominate in both services. However, Lexis-Nexis also provides access to a substantial number of French materials, in particular decisions of the *Cour de cassation* and *Conseil d'Etat* from about 1970, as well as to legislative and quasi-legislative material published in the French Official Journal (*Journal Officiel*) and some other French materials. Some foreign and European Community materials (French cases, the Official Journal of the European Communities) are also available in a CD-ROM format, but probably not widely available in American libraries because there is some duplication with LEXIS. However, the researcher looking for recent (post 1980) periodical articles will find the LEGALTRAC base on CD-ROM of considerable help. A final word of warning: some data bases or the "hosts" providing access will not recognize letters with accents and the like (é, g, ä, ¯n, etc.); other may reproduce such letters in garbled fashion.

ii.　Printed Sources
a.　*Materials in English*

The reader wishing to get an introduction to the law of a particular country may be able to rely on a number of good one or two volume books, some of which have been mentioned before. Examples include E.J. Cohn et al., Manual of German Law (2d ed. 1968-71), obviously no longer up-to-date, but still valuable for many purposes; N. Horn, H. Kötz & G. Leser, German Private and Commercial Law, An Introduction (T. Weir trans., 1982) (newer but still without many recent developments); Amos and Walton's Introduction to French Law (F. H. Lawson, A. E. Anton & L. N. Brown eds., 3d ed. 1967) (good as a basic introduction but lacking many recent materials as well); M. Cappelletti, J. H. Merryman & J. M. Perillo, The Italian Legal System—An Introduction (1967) (same); G. L. Certoma, The Italian Legal System (1985) (same). More recent are a series of single country guides published by Kluwer: T. Ansay & D. Wallace, Introduction to Turkish Law (3d ed. 1996); J.M.J. Chorus et al., Introduction to Dutch Law for Foreign Lawyers (2d rev. ed. 1993); F. Dessemontet & T. Ansay, Introduction to Swiss Law (2d ed. 1995); K. J. Kerameus & Ph. J. Kozyris, Introduction to Greek Law (2d rev. ed. 1993); and A. Shapira & K. C. DeWitt-Arar, Introduction to the Law of Israel (1995).

Shorter introductions to the law of individual countries can be found for instance in the "country reports" in volume 1 of the (still incomplete) International Encyclopedia of Comparative Law, and even more summary ones in the

73

"foreign law" volumes of the Martindale-Hubbell Lawyers Directory. If the research is to be limited to European countries, the "Doing Business in Europe" portion of the CCH Common Market Reporter will provide country summaries organized on a largely consistent scheme that are updated from time to time. Many of the items mentioned here also contain bibliographies useful for further research.

The reader wanting to do detailed research using English language materials will (unless concentrating on the very recent past) be well advised to begin with the late Prof. Ch. Szladits' multi-volume: "Bibliography on Foreign and Comparative Law Materials in English." The first volume covers the period 1790 to 1953, and subsequent volumes the periods to 1983. Further volumes, compiled by V. Pechota, cover the period 1984 to 1990. Entries are arranged by topic and numbered, but, by an ingenious system of cross references to these numbers, the researcher can easily focus on an individual country as well. Bibliographies in the American Journal of Comparative Law supplemented the basic volumes between updates by additional volumes, but unfortunately work on this valuable research aid appears to have been discontinued.

Bibliographies on specific topics appear from time to time in the "International Lawyer" published by the American Bar Association Section on International Law and Practice. Some excellent examples include G. C. Heinrich, Funds Transfers, Payments, and Payment Systems—International Initiatives Towards Legal Harmonization, 28 Int'l Law. 787 (1994); and P. Winship, The U. N. Sales Convention: A Bibliography of English-Language Publications, 28 Int'l Law. 401 (1994). The "Regional Developments" section of the same publication is sometimes useful for the purpose of updating more comprehensive information found in other sources. The topic-oriented volumes of the International Encyclopedia of Comparative Law, to the extent available, will often furnish a detailed initial guide for comparative work on a specific topic, but in assessing their currency the reader must obviously bear in mind the widely differing publication dates of the various items contained in the Encyclopedia.

If the researcher is looking for statutes, cases, and the like, then many of the larger law libraries will have certain of the basic materials of countries with a common-law heritage, such as the United Kingdom, Canada, or Australia. Use of these materials is explained in the standard texts on legal research and need not be repeated here. The researcher should not forget in this context that English may be at least a second official language in some areas, such as India. Thus statute and case materials from that country are available in English and are organized and indexed more or less on English lines.

For some non-English speaking countries, there are translations of the civil and sometimes other (commercial, criminal, etc.) codes. Sources include M. Beltramo, G. E. Longo and J. H. Merryman, The Italian Civil Code (rev. ed., 2 vols. 1991–1996); J. H. Crabb, the French Civil Code (rev. ed. 1995); S. L. Goren, The German Civil Code (rev. ed. 1992); and S. L. Goren & I. S. Forrester, The German Commercial Code (1979). Unfortunately, the time it takes to complete, edit, and publish such translations is usually fairly long so that even works with a very recent publication date may, in fact, not be up to date, and time between edition is, for obvious commercial reasons, usually also long (but note that the edition of the Italian Civil Code relies on separate pamphlets in a binder, which facilitates quicker updating).

The usefulness of these translations for research is also somewhat limited because they tend to lack references to pertinent auxiliary statutes, not to mention court decisions. English translations of some especially significant shorter foreign materials (statutes, treaties, cases), with an often helpful introductory note, appear from time to time in the American Society of International Law's publication "International Legal Materials" (I.L.M.) (to which a number of references have been made in this book). I.L.M. also contains lists of actions concerning treaties to which the United States is a party and, even more valuable for the researcher, since that material is, of course, not contained in the United States Department of State's Annual "Treaties in Force," lists of actions concerning treaties to which the United States is not a party. Finally, the Louisiana State Law Institute publication of translations of two major classical multi-volume French treatises, those of Planiol and Aubry & Rau, merits mention. The translations were made on the basis of relatively old editions of these works and thus are not a reliable guide to the current state of French law, but are a good indication of the general organizational scheme of a standard work on "civil law." The reader using translations should, however, again be reminded of the special problems, mentioned in chapter IX, section 1, which are posed by translated legal materials.

Since English is one of the official languages of the European Community/European Union, official materials issued in that context are available in English translation and there is a most extensive body of books and articles in English, including several specialized periodicals (Common Market Law Review, European Law Review, etc.). An adequate research guide would exceed the purposes of these pages, but the following items provide a great deal of useful information: M. J. Raisch, The European Union, A Selective Research Guide, 1 Colum. J. Eur. L. 149 (1995), supplemented by J. Streil & J. Suter, Research Guide for United States Users to

Materials From the Court of Justice of the European Communities, 1 Colum. J. Eur. L. 559 (1995). Both items also contain information on electronic research, but given the rapid pace of change in this field that information needs some updating.

b.   *Foreign language materials.*

The researcher with some foreign language ability will find that such an ability is useful even beyond the possibility of doing research in the law of the countries where the particular language is current.   A number of foreign periodicals, especially, of course, those specializing in comparative or international law (such as Rabel's Zeitschrift or IPrax in Germany, the Revue Internationale de Droit Comparé, the Revue critique de droit international privé, and the Journal du Droit International (often referred to as "Clunet") in France, and many others, publish not only articles but also new legislation, court decisions, bibliographic materials, etc., covering a wide variety of countries.

In many civil-law countries, there are unannotated, frequently updated, versions of the major codes published primarily for law students.   They are useful for fast introductory research and to obtain a very current text. Any more detailed research will, however, require the use of an annotated code or "commentary" for a code (or a similar work for a major statute—an example might be the German statute on stock corporations *[Aktiengesetz]*—which is not technically a Code[2]).   Annotated codes contain cross-references to relevant provisions in other codes, references (or full-text

---

[2]The French publisher Dalloz even sells an annotated edition of the French statute of July 24, 1966, on commercial "companies" which covers essentially all forms of business entities under the title *Code des Societes* (Companies Code) although the statute in question is not officially a code at all.

77

reprints) for pertinent auxiliary statutes, summaries of court decisions, and citations to scholarly articles.

In commentaries to the codes, on the other hand, the text of the individual code articles is followed by comments by learned authors, but, of course, these comments will also cite relevant books, articles, and court decisions as well as related statutory materials. An example of annotated codes would be the French Civil, Commercial, etc., codes in the Petits Codes Dalloz series, an example of a "Commentary" type code would be the Palandt edition of the German Civil Code, all of these items having been frequently cited in this work. The researcher looking for fairly specialized legislation or administrative regulations will sometimes find that they are not available in the standard privately published sources. However, most countries also publish some type of "official gazette," often looking somewhat like the Federal Register (which appears to have been modeled to some extent on them), that publishes all official legislative and quasi-legislative materials, and sometimes committee reports and other legislative materials as well.[3] Examples are, e.g., the French *Journal Officiel* (*J.O.*), the German (and the somewhat differently organized Austrian) *Bundesgesetzblatt* (*BGBl*)[4], the Italian *Gazetta Ufficiale,* the Swiss *Bundesblatt/Feuille Fédérale,* etc.

In some countries, the governmental publishing office, which publishes these, also publishes a compiled collection of statutes which includes, arranged by topic, all substantial

---

[3]Official and unofficial publications of statutes sometimes give, in a footnote, references to such legislative history materials.

[4]The German (but not the Austrian) publication is divided into a part I for new legislative materials and a part II for new treaties. (Hence the Roman numerals I or II included in a cite to this publication in this book.) The collection of compiled statutes mentioned in the next following lines in the text is considered as a part III and thus cited BGBl III.

legislation currently in effect, with later amendments of earlier statutes inserted in their proper place.

General case finding systems along the lines of the American Digest System are generally unknown outside the common-law orbit, but works collecting summaries of cases, arranged in the order of a particular statute, or works collecting such summaries for a particular field of law may exist. Also largely unknown are general article finders such as the Index to Legal Periodicals and the Index to Foreign Legal Periodicals.[5]

On the other hand, the researcher will find that in addition to a number of periodicals (sometimes of a weekly nature) reproducing articles and often also court decisions and even legislation of a general legal interest, there are, in civil law countries, many specialized law reviews that are valuable research aids because they contain not only articles but also, quite generally, cases (in full with comments or, at least, in abstract form), new legislation, bibliographic materials, and related information. They are thus useful not only for a deeper understanding of complex issues through their articles but also for the current information they contain. The French *Revue critique de droit international privé,* for instance, provides, in addition to scholarly articles, coverage of French (and sometimes other) cases in the area of its concern, but also references to new legislation, an annual bibliography listing articles in major periodicals published in a variety of countries, and tables indicating the status (signatures, ratifications, reservations, etc.) of the conventions sponsored by the Hague Conference of Private International Law, of the

---

[5]The latter is useful also for finding material on foreign law in some American publications, because it indexes a number of publications (in particular a number of the law school-related international journals) that the Index to Legal Periodicals does not index.

Brussels and Lugano Jurisdiction and Judgments Conventions, of the Rome Convention on the Law Applicable to Contracts, etc.

3. CITATION

The primary goal of citation is to enable readers to access the sources upon which the author relied. Improper citation impedes this goal and, in turn, diminishes the impact of the author's thesis. Therefore, it is absolutely critical for the student to master the rules of citation.[6] Quite simply, proper citation is an indication that the writer is a thorough researcher, knowledgeable in the area in which she writes; poor citation, however, leaves the impression that the writer is careless and raises concerns about the writer's trustworthiness.

In addition to the reasons listed above, an author's use of proper citation, or the lack thereof, is often a factor that legal journals consider when making publication decisions. Between two articles of comparable substantive value, a journal editor is much more likely to choose the article that displays flawless citation because correcting poor citation is a cumbersome and time-consuming process.

1.   Overview of *The Bluebook*

The Bluebook is organized into three large sections: (1) the "Bluepages," or special rules for citation in court documents; (2) the general rules of citation; and (3) various reference tables and indices. First, the student should thoroughly familiarize herself with the front and back covers of *The Bluebook*, which provide examples of the most commonly used citation forms with cross-references to the related rules

---

[6]All references in this section are taken from *The Bluebook: A Uniform System of Citation* (Columbia Law Review Ass'n et al. eds., 18th ed. 2005) For an excellent electronic resource on proper citation (in both *Bluebook* and *ALWD* formats), see Peter W. Martin, Introduction to Basic Legal Citation (LII 2007 ed.), http://www.law.cornell.edu/citation/ (last visited Feb. 9, 2008).

explaining the citation form. The back cover provides examples for court documents and memoranda, whereas the front cover displays examples for law review footnotes.

The first nine rules of *The Bluebook* address general rules of citation and style. Areas addressed by Rules 1–9 include structure and use of citations; permissible typefaces for law reviews; proper citation of subdivisions; short citation forms; quotations; abbreviations, numerals and symbols; italicization; capitalization; and titles of judges, officials, and terms of court.[7] The last twelve rules cover specific rules for citing various types of primary and secondary authority. In Rules 10–21, the writer will find the proper format for citing cases; constitutions; statutes; legislative materials; administrative and executive materials; books, reports, and nonperiodic materials; periodical materials; unpublished and forthcoming sources; electronic media and nonprint resources; services; foreign materials; and international materials.[8]

Following the rules of citation, sixteen reference tables appear, which provide supplementary information about various details of citation and abbreviation that are mentioned throughout the rules. These tables instruct the writer regarding either the proper citation format or the accepted abbreviation for such things as U.S. federal and state jurisdictions, foreign jurisdictions, intergovernmental organizations, treaty sources, arbitral reporters, case names, court names, explanatory phrases, legislative documents, geographical terms, judges and officials, months, periodicals, publishing terms, services, and subdivisions. As these tables supplement the rules, the thorough writer must refer to both the rules and the related tables continually throughout the writing process.

---

[7] *See Bluebook, supra* note 17, at 45–78.
[8] *See id.* at 79–192.

2. Rules of Style

a. Typeface

Unlike court documents and legal memoranda, legal journals and law reviews utilize specific fonts and typeface conventions. Furthermore, these rules apply differently depending on whether text is in the main body of the article or in a footnote. Because the pursuit of publication is one of the goals of academic legal writing, these rules should also be observed in seminar papers. Rule 2 of *The Bluebook* covers these issues.

In seminar papers, students should use traditional fonts throughout, such as the Times New Roman font used in this book.[9] In addition to font choice, most journals and law reviews use three different typefaces in citations: Plain Text, *Italics*, and LARGE AND SMALL CAPITALS.[10] The rules for applying these typefaces vary depending on the type of authority that is cited. For example, italic typeface is used for explanatory phrases, introductory signals, case names in short citation form, case names and procedural phrases that appear in the main text, and in instances where the author is adding emphasis to quoted material.[11] In contrast, the large and small capitals typeface is used for books (both the author and the title) and periodicals.

It is important to remember that each one of the rules of citation (Rules 10-21) indicates the appropriate typeface for that authority. Accordingly, the student must consult both

---

[9]*Id.* at 54.

[10]*Id.*

[11]If the author chooses to use italics to emphasize quoted material, she must indicate that she has added emphasis by including a parenthetical at the end of the citation. For example: "Roe v. Wade, 410 U.S. 113, 116 (1973) (emphasis added)." *Id.* at 69.

Rule 2 and the various rules of citation to ensure that the proper typeface is used.

b. Structure of citations and signals

In seminar papers, citations always appear in footnotes on the same page as the text to which they refer. The footnote should appear at the end of the sentence only if the entire sentence is supported by the cited authority;[12] if the authority supports only a portion of the sentence, place the footnote immediately after the portion of the sentence that it supports.[13] Footnotes should always appear after punctuation, with the exception of dashes and colons.[14]

In general, cited authority attempts to accomplish one of four main tasks: (1) to support the proposition in the text; (2) to compare authorities; (3) to contradict a proposition; and (4) to provide background information.[15] In a seminar paper, the student must use introductory signals to indicate to the reader the category in which the authority has been placed. Rule 1.2 of *The Bluebook* addresses this issue.

First, Signals used to cite authority that supports the author's proposition include *E.g., Accord, See, See also,* and *Cf.* To compare two different authorities, the signal *Compare ___ with ___* is used. To indicate contradiction, use *Contra, But see,* and *But cf.* All signals are italicized. The meaning of each introductory signal—even those within the same category—differ significantly from each other. Accordingly, you must consult Rule 1.2 before including a signal. If using multiple signals within the same category, they must appear

---

[12]*Id.* at 45.
[13]*Id.*
[14]*Id.*
[15]*Id.* at 46.

in the order enumerated above.[16]

In addition, if using numerous authorities within the same signal, they must be placed in the following order: (1) constitutions; (2) statutes; (3) treaties and international agreements; (4) cases; (5) legislative materials; (6) administrative and executive materials; (7) resolutions, decisions, and regulations of intergovernmental organizations; (8) records, briefs and petitions; and (9) secondary materials.[17]

Immediately after citing authority, use parentheticals to explain the relevance of the authority to the proposition indicated in the text. Parenthetical text should always begin with a present participial phrase.[18] For example:

> *See generally* Akhil Reed Amar, *Reports of My Death Are Greatly Exaggerated: A Reply*, 138 U. PA. L. REV. 1651 (1990) (arguing that the author and the two-tier theory of federal jurisdiction are still viable)

Finally, remember that if the signal is used as a verb in a textual sentence, it is not italicized.[19]

c.   Short citation forms

When citing authority, in many instances it is permissible to use a shortened version of the original citation form. Each one of the rules of citation provides a short citation format for the authority that it addresses. Accordingly, the writer must consult each of these rules to determine the appropriate rule of citation in each case. General principles of short citation forms, however, are found in Rule 4.

In addition to specific short citation forms found in the

---

[16] *Id.* at 48.
[17] *Id.* at 48–51.
[18] *Id.* at 51.
[19] *Id.* at 47–48.

rules of citation, Rule 4 addresses three generic short forms: "*Id.*," "*supra*," and "Hereinafter." "*Id.*" may be used in two situations: (1) when citing the immediately preceding authority within the same footnote; or (2) when citing the immediately preceding footnote when the footnote contains only one authority. [20] If the subsequent "*Id.*" citation refers to a different section of the preceding authority (e.g., a different page) indicate the difference in the footnote.[21] For example:

[1]   Chalfin v. Specter, 233 A.2d 562, 562 (Pa. 1967).
[2]   *Id.* at 563.
[3]   42 U.S.C. § 1983 (1994)
[4]   *See id.* § 1981.

"*Id.*" cannot be used to refer to an authority in a preceding footnote if the preceding footnote has more than one source.[22] This rule is ignored, however, for sources in parentheticals, explanatory phrases, or prior/subsequent history.[23] For example:

[1]   Tuten v. United States, 460 U.S. 660, 663 (1983) (quoting Ralston v. Robinson, 454 U.S. 201, 206) (1981)).
[2]   *See id.* at 664.

"*Supra*" and "hereinafter" may be used only to refer to certain types of authority: legislative hearings, books, pamphlets, reports, unpublished materials, nonprint resources, periodicals, services, treaties and international agreements, regulations, directives, decisions of intergovernmental organizations, and internal cross-

---

[20] *Id.* at 64.
[21] *Id.*
[22] *Id.*
[23] *Id.* at 65.

references.[24] In general, these short forms may *not* be used for cases, statutes, constitutions, legislative materials, restatements, model codes, or regulations.[25]

"*Supra*" is used to refer back to authority that has already been fully cited in a previous section of the article. "Hereinafter," on the other hand, is a customized form of short citation that allows the author to provide a shortened name for a particular authority that will be used throughout the work. When choosing between these forms, do not use "hereinafter" when "*supra*" would suffice.[26] For example:

> [1]*Proposed Amendments to the Federal Rules of Criminal Procedure: Hearings Before the Subcomm. on Criminal Justice of the H. Comm. on the Judiciary*, 95th Cong. 92–93 (1977) [hereinafter *Hearings*] (testimony of Prof. Wayne LaFave).

d.   Quotations

The rules for proper quotation are arguably the most complex among the rules of style and one of the most common areas of error. Rule 5 of *The Bluebook*, which addresses quotations, is divided into three sections: (1) formatting of quotations; (2) alterations and quotations within quotations; and (3) omissions.

In general, quotations are treated differently depending on (1) whether the quote is more or less than fifty words and (2) whether the quotation appears in the text or in footnotes. For quotations of fifty or more words:

- In the text: indented on both the left and right sides, without quotation marks, but preserve internal

---

[24]*Id.* at 66.
[25]*Id.*
[26]*Id.* at 66–67.

quotation marks, if any. Footnote numbers should be placed immediately after the final punctuation of the quotation.[27]

- In footnotes: the same rules apply as in the text, with the exception that citations to the quoted authority should not be placed immediately after the punctuation, but rather should be placed on the next line down, flush against the left margin.[28]

For example, in the main text a quotation is formatted as follows:

> Commentators have argued that humanistic principles should be applied to migratory issues. According to Gabor and Rosenquest:
>
> > Understanding the overall problem of migration requires applying a humanistic perspective to the major causes of human migration. A recognized foundation of the present-day international legal order is that human beings who share a common cultural, linguistic, and ethnic heritage live together in recognition of their inherent right of self-determination. This realization is the basis for the recognition of state sovereignty. The ever-widening gap between the socioeconomic and ideological development of sovereign nation-states in the world community creates the basic source of tension.[1]

The same quotation in a footnote is formatted as follows:

> [1] Commentators have argued that humanistic principles should be applied to migratory issues. According to Gabor and Rosenquest:

---

[27] *Id.* at 68–69.
[28] *Id.*

> Understanding the overall problem of migration requires applying a humanistic perspective to the major causes of human migration. A recognized foundation of the present-day international legal order is that human beings who share a common cultural, linguistic, and ethnic heritage live together in recognition of their inherent right of self-determination. This realization is the basis for the recognition of state sovereignty. The ever-widening gap between the socioeconomic and ideological development of sovereign nation-states in the world community creates the basic source of tension.

Francis Gabor & John B. Rosenquest, *The Unsettled Status of Economic Refugees from the American and International Legal Perspectives - A Proposal for Recognition Under Existing International Law*, 41 TEX. INT'L L.J. 275, 276 (2006).

For quotes of forty-nine or fewer words, do not set off from the rest of the text.[29] Rather, enclose the quotation in quotation marks and use single quotation marks (e.g., 'single quotations') for quotations within the quotation.[30]

e.   Alterations

When altering letters or substituting words in a quotation, indicate the substituted material in brackets: "[P]ublic confidence in the [adversary] system depend[s upon] full disclosure of all the facts."[31]   Also, changes to cited material (e.g., alterations, omissions of citations, addition of emphasis) must be noted in parentheticals.[32]

---

[29] *Id.* at 69.
[30] *Id.*
[31] *Id.* at 69.
[32] *Id.* at 69–70.

f.   Omissions

Use an ellipsis to indicate omitted words in a quotation. The proper format of an ellipsis *always* consists of four spaces (noted here by the use of underline marks) and three periods ("_._._._").[33]   Modern word processing programs with autocorrect features will often transform an ellipsis typed by the drafter into a symbol; this "corrected" version is, in fact, usually incorrect because it does not observe proper spacing between the periods. Students should, therefore, ensure that autocorrecting features are disabled for the ellipsis.[34]

An ellipsis should never be used to begin a quotation or to indicate altered words.[35] In addition, a period may be added to an ellipsis to indicate punctuation in the original quotation. The addition of a period, or the alteration of the ellipsis in general, depends on what portion of the material is omitted. A quick reference for omissions is as follows:

- Beginning of sentence omitted: capitalize the first letter and place it in brackets (if not already capitalized).[36]
- Middle of the sentence omitted: _._._._[37]
- End of a sentence omitted: _._._._.[38]
- Language *after* the end of a sentence is omitted: ._._._._[39]
- Language both *at the end* and *after the end* of the sentence is omitted: _._._._._[40]

Because the rules for quotations, alterations, and

---

[33] *Id.* at 70.

[34] Similarly, autocorrect features may also reformat ordinals ("9th") into superscript ("9th"). Rule 6.2 prohibits the use of superscript for ordinals. *See id.* at 74.

[35] *Id.* at 70.

[36] *Id.* at 71.

[37] *Id.*

[38] *Id.*

[39] *Id.*

[40] *Id.*

omissions are complex, the student should refer to Rule 5 of *The Bluebook* each time a quotation is inserted.

g. Other rules of style

In addition to the rules explained above, the student should also be aware of and consult frequently the remaining rules of style. These rules address such situations as abbreviations, numerals, and symbols (Rule 6); italicization in special circumstances (Rule 7); capitalization (Rule 8); and proper titles of judges, officials, and terms of court (Rule 9).

3. Rules of Citation

a. Cases

Because of their weight as primary authority and highly persuasive secondary authority, cases constitute a large portion of the citations in scholarly papers. As a result, the requirements for citing cases in Rule 10 are complex and depend on a variety of factors.

In general, a full case citation should include: (1) the name of the case; (2) the published sources in which it may be found; (3) a parenthetical indicating the court and jurisdiction; (4) date or year of the decision; and (5) subsequent history of the case, if any.[41] For example, in a footnote:

> 1   United States v. MacDonald, 531 F.2d 196, 199–200 (4th Cir. 1976) (resting review of the dispositive issue on the principle of judicial economy), *rev'd*, 435 U.S. 850 (1978).

In case citations, always abbreviate any word that

---

[41] In some circumstances, case citations may require additional parenthetical information, prior history of the case, and special forms for pending and unreported cases. *See generally id.* at 91–97.

appears in Table 6.[42] Furthermore, always abbreviate states, countries, and other geographical units in Table 10, unless the geographical unit is the entire named of the party (e.g., "United States"). For example:

> Center for Nat'l Sec. Studies v. U.S. Dep't of Justice Alvarez-Machain v. United States

For cases that are available in more than one reporter series, cite to the reporter series indicated in Table 1. For example, if citing a Supreme Court decision, Table 1 requires citation to United States Reports (U.S.) if available; otherwise cite to the Supreme Court Reporter (S. Ct.), the United States Supreme Court Reporters, Lawyers' Edition (L. Ed.), or the United States Law Week (U.S.L.W.), in that order. Table 1 also provides the required reporter series for all other federal and state courts.

From time to time, the student may need to cite to unreported cases. These cases are usually available in online databases such as LexisNexis and Westlaw before they are published in reporters. To cite to unreported cases available on electronic databases, provide the case name, docket number, database identifier, court name, and full date of the most recent major disposition of the case.[43] Page numbers must be preceded by an asterisk.[44] For example:

> Gibbs v. Frank, No. 02-3924, 2004 U.S. App. LEXIS 21357, at *18 (3d Cir. Oct. 14, 2004).

> Shelton v. City of Manhattan Beach, No. B171606, 2004 WL 2163741, at *1 (Cal. Ct. App. Sept. 28, 2004).

---

[42] *See generally id.* at 335–37.
[43] *Id.* at 95–96.
[44] *Id.* at 96.

Finally, cases may be cited in short form in two circumstances: (1) the case has already been cited in the same footnote; or (2) the case has been cited in full form, short form, or by use of *Id.*, in one of the five footnotes immediately preceding the current footnote.[45] In general, short case forms feature a shorter version of one party's name, the volume number and abbreviation of the reporter, and the cited page.[46] Short forms are italicized in footnotes.[47] For example:

> 1   Birl v. Estelle, 660 F.2d 592 (5th Cir. Nov. 1981).
> 2   United States v. Martinez-Fuerte, 428 U.S. 543, 557 (1976); Cal. Bankers Ass'n v. Shultz, 416 U.S. 21, 62 (1974).
> 3   *In re* Draughon Training Inst., Inc., 119 B.R. 921, 926 (Bankr. W.D. La. 1990).
> 4   *Birl,* 660 F.2d at 595.

If the case has not been cited in any of the five immediately preceding footnotes, it must be cited in full.[48]

b.   Constitutions

Rule 11 governs the citation of the U.S. and state constitutions. In footnotes, include either "U.S." or the state abbreviation (Table 10) and the word CONST., both elements in large and small capitals, and the subdivision cited (abbreviated according to Table 16).[49] In the main text, differentiate between the U.S. Constitution and state constitutions by capitalizing subdivisions and traditional names in the U.S. Constitution.[50] For example:

U.S. CONST. art. IV, § 1

---

[45] *Id.* at 97–98.
[46] *Id.* at 98.
[47] *Id.*
[48] *Id.* at 97.
[49] *Id.* at 100.
[50] *Id.*

Article IV
Full Faith and Credit Clause

TENN. CONST., art. I, § 10
article 1, section 10
double jeopardy clause

c.   Statutes

The citation of statutes is governed by Rule 12. In general, the citation should include the title number, the abbreviation of the code cited, the section symbol ("§") and section number, and the date of the code edition cited.[51] If citing a codified Act, include the official name of the Act.[52] If the statute is no longer in force, cite to the current official or unofficial code if the statute still appears there.[53] Always include a parenthetical indicating whether a statute has been invalidated, repealed, or amended.[54] Abbreviate all federal and state statutes according to Table 1.

d.   Secondary Sources

In addition to primary sources, the student writer should cite to secondary sources to support the propositions advanced in her seminar paper. Secondary sources cover a wide array of materials, including books, periodicals, journals, newspapers, electronic media, and international sources. Rules 15, 16, 18, 20, and 21 govern these sources.

Books

In citing books, include the author's full name, title of the book, the page cited, the editor's full name and the "ed." or

---

[51] *Id.* at 101.
[52] *See id.*
[53] *Id.* at 102.
[54] *Id.* at 102–03.

"trans." abbreviation (if edited or translated), the name of the publisher, the year of the edition cited, and the year of the original publication.[55] The author's name and the title of the book should be in large and small capitals:

> CHARLES DICKENS, BLEAK HOUSE 50 (Norman Page ed., Penguin Books 1971) (1853).

Rule 15.8 also provides special citation forms for frequently cited works such as legal dictionaries, encyclopedias, Federalist papers, and so forth.

Periodicals / Journals / Newspapers

Periodical materials, whether journals, magazines, newspapers, or other sources, follow the same generic format. The student must be careful to ensure that the proper typeface is utilized, as typefaces commonly change multiple times even within the same citation. When citing periodicals, include the author's full name, the title of the article (in italics), the journal volume number (if any), the abbreviation or name of the journal (in large and small capitals), the page on which the article begins, the span of pages cited, the date of publication, and a parenthetical describing the content if necessary.[56] For example:

> Charles A. Reich, *The New Property*, 73 YALE L.J. 733, 737–38 (1964) (discussing the importance of government largess).

> Robert J. Samuelson, *A Slow Fix for the Banks*, NEWSWEEK, Feb. 18, 1991, at 55.

> Seth Mydans, *Los Angeles Police Chief Removed for 60 Days in Inquiry on Beating*, N.Y. TIMES,

---

[55] *See id.* at 129.
[56] *Id.* at 138–39.

Apr. 5, 1991, at A1.

Periodicals are abbreviated according to Table 13 (specific periodical abbreviations) and Table 10 (geographic abbreviations).[57] Also, in the case of citing student works, be sure to include the designation of the piece (e.g., comment, note, or recent development) before the title of the work to clearly indicate that it is student-written:

> B. George Ballman, Jr., Note, *Amended Rule 6.1: Another Move Towards Mandatory Pro Bono? Is That What We Want?*, 7 GEO. J. LEGAL ETHICS 1139, 1162 (1994).

Electronic media

Citations to electronic media are most frequently used when citing to unreported cases or internet sources. In general, if the source is available both in traditional printed form and electronically, the student should cite to the printed source.[58] Two exceptions to this general rule apply: (1) the source is unavailable in printed form; or (2) the source is available but an internet source is identical to the printed version and the citation to the internet source will substantially improve access to the material.[59]

First, all internet citations should feature the internet address, or "URL," that will most readily point readers directly to the cited source.[60] If the URL is straightforward, cite it in its entirety; if it will result in an incredibly long and complex citation, cite to the main URL and include a parenthetical explaining to the reader how to access the information:

---

[57] *Id.; see also id.* at 349–72 (Table 13); *id.* at 343–47 (Table 10).

[58] *Id.* at 153.

[59] *Id.* at 153–54.

[60] *Id.* at 154.

http://fjsrc.urban.org/noframe/wqs/q_data_1.htm#20
01
(follow "2001:AOUSC out" hyperlink; then follow
"Offenses: TTSECMSO" hyperlink).

If the internet document is available in both the
internet .HTML format and a format that preserves pagination
and attributes such as the Adobe .PDF format, cite to the
latter source so that the reader may access the information
more easily:

> U.S. Citizenship and Immigration Services Fact
> Sheet: Guatemalan Asylum Applicants in the
> Context of the ABC Settlement Agreement and
> Section 203 of the Nicaraguan Adjustment and
> Central American Relief Act (NACARA) (Feb.
> 28,2007),
> http://www.uscis.gov/files/pressrelease/Guate
> malanAsylum022807.pdf.

When a source is available in both print form and on
the internet, and an internet citation would substantially
improve access to the information, include a parallel citation
to the internet source after the print citation, separating the
two with the "*available at*" explanatory phrase:

> Am. Mining Cong. v. U.S. Army Corps of Eng'rs,
> No. CIV.A. 93-1754 SSH (D.D.C. Jan. 23, 1997),
> *available   at*
> http://www.wetlands.com/fed/tulloch1.htm.

When an electronic source is undated, indicate the date
that the website was last visited in a parenthetical after the
URL:

> U.S. Department of Justice Home Page,
> http://www.usdoj.gov/ (last visited Jan. 22,
> 2007).

Because the standards for citing internet sources are far more complex than is reasonably possible to address in a general overview, the student should always refer to Rule 18 when drafting these citations.

e. International Sources

For the student of transnational law, international sources will comprise a significant portion of citations present in the seminar paper. Table 2 provides specific citation examples for each international jurisdiction and is considered the primary source for such citations. When Table 2 does not adequately address an issue, or the source to be cited is not analogous to an example provided therein, Rules 20 and 21 provide important guidance for the proper citation of international sources.

Foreign materials

First, Rule 20 addresses generic issues of citation for foreign materials, such as: (1) citation when the jurisdiction is not evident from the context; (2) the use of non-English-language documents; (3) the proper citation of cases, constitutions and statutes; (4) non-English-language and foreign periodicals; and (5) short citation forms. In most cases, Rule 20 directs the student to cite these sources according to the most analogous citation rule (e.g., foreign cases cited according to Rule 10), but also provides additional instructions where necessary.[61]

International Materials

The proper citation of international materials is governed by Rule 21. This rule provides basic citation forms

---

[61] *See generally id.* at 164–67.

for the most common international materials. Students should refer to the first two pages of this rule for numerous examples of proper citations.

Rule 21 is divided into six general sections: (1) treaties and other international agreements (Rule 21.4); (2) international law cases (Rule 21.5); (3) international arbitrations (Rule 21.6); (4) United Nations materials (Rule 21.7); European Union materials (Rule 21.8.2); and World Trade Organization materials (Rule 21.8.4).

For treaties, two different rules apply in Rule 21.4, depending on the number of parties to the treaty. For treaties among three or fewer parties, include the name of the agreement, the abbreviated names of the parties to the agreement, the subdivision cited (if any), the date of signing, and one U.S. treaty source:

> Treaty of Friendship, Commerce and Navigation, U.S.-Japan, art. X, Apr. 2, 1953, 4 U.S.T. 2063.

In the case of treaties among more than three parties, include the name of the agreement, the subdivision cited, the date of signing, one U.S. treaty source, and one international source:

> Geneva Convention Relative to the Treatment of Prisoners of War art. 3, Aug. 12, 1949, 6 U.S.T. 3316, 75 U.N.T.S. 135.

The citation of international cases generally follows Rule 10, but is modified by Rule 21.5 to include special rules for certain courts. These courts include, but are not limited to the International Court of Justice, the Permanent Court of International Justice, the European Union courts, the European Court of Human Rights, the Inter-American Commission on Human Rights, the East African Court of

Appeal, International Criminal Tribunals, among others.[62] International arbitrations are also governed by Rule 21.5, with some modifications indicated in Rule 21.6.

The proper citation of United Nations sources can refer either to the Official Record or to internet sources, but Rule 21.7 indicates a strong preference for the United Nations webpage, http://www.un.org.[63] Moreover, the rule specifically indicates certain disfavored sources, such as yearbooks, periodicals, mimeographed documents, or sales documents, which should only be cited when absolutely necessary.[64] Finally citations to the United Nations charter should be formatted as follows:

U.N. Charter art. 2, para. 4.

Rule 21.8 addresses the citation of materials of various intergovernmental organizations, including the League of Nations, the European Union and European Community, the Council of Europe, and the World Trade Organization. For materials outside of these specific categories, cite by analogy to United Nations materials (Rule 21.7) and to the specific forms enumerated in Rule 21.8.[65]

The remainder of Rule 21 addresses minutiae in international sources, including international non-governmental organizations (Rule 21.9), yearbooks (Rule 21.10), digests (Rule 21.11), and short citation forms (Rule 21.12).

---

[62]See *id.* at 174–78.
[63]*See id.* at 179.
[64]*See id.*
[65]*Id.* at 189–90.

Conclusion

Without a doubt, the rules of proper citation are quite complex and difficult to master. This short guide to *The Bluebook* does not attempt to cover every rule, but rather its purpose is to provide an overview of proper citation. Because of the intricacy of the rules, students should not attempt to memorize the nuances of each and every one.

Rather, the student must keep a copy of *The Bluebook* close at hand, must refer to it constantly during the writing process, and should not hesitate to look up the rule for each and every type of authority that is cited. Through practice, the student's proficiency and comfort level will increase greatly.

4.   PUBLISHING THE SEMINAR PAPER

Once you've finished the seminar paper, consider the possibility of publishing it. As you've already done a large portion of the work it would take to publish an article, you might want to get an extra credential for it.

Publishing your paper might be easier than you think.[66] With a little extra work, such as adding background and introductory material, there are many law reviews and specialty journals that might be willing to publish your article. They are constantly in search of good quality legal scholarship.

Your professor is certain to have published articles in journals and law reviews, ask him for advice on the publication process. It might even be worthwhile to tell your professor before you begin writing your seminar paper of your intentions to publish it when the seminar is completed. Your plans could have a bearing on your choice of topic.

---

[66] For additional tips on publishing student papers, see VOLOKH, *supra* note 1, at 185–206; FAJANS & FALK, *supra* note 2, at 172–74.

V. SAMPLES OF TRANSNATIONAL LEGAL WRITING

1. *The Quest for Transformation to a Market Economy: Privatization and Foreign Investment in Hungary*

---

24 VAND. J. TRANSNAT'L L. 269 (1991)

FRANCIS A. GABOR[*]

I. INTRODUCTION

Since 1988, Hungary has experienced political and socio-economic changes of unprecedented dimensions. By March 1990, a deepening economic crisis led in large part to Hungary's first free, multi-party elections. Suddenly, forty years of domination by Marxist ideology and political structure were swept aside by the political self-determination of the Hungarian people. A new constitutional democracy emerged almost overnight and provided a model for other states in Central and Eastern Europe.

Sweeping socio-economic changes, however, have not accompanied political freedom. Transformation to a free market economic system has become the most challenging and time consuming task for the Hungarian people and their freely elected government. From a historical perspective, the Hungarian people always have considered themselves part of Western civilization and defenders of both the civilization and its values. The model for transformation today, therefore, still is found in the Western European free market economic system, which is based on pluralist constitutional democracy.

---

[*] Professor of Law, Memphis State University. D.Jur., 1967, Eotvos L. Science University (Hung.); J.D. 1975, Tulane University; LL.M., 1973, University of California, Berkeley. The writing of this Article was supported by a Fulbright research grant provided by the United States Information Agency.

103

The successful process of economic transformation must be based on the revitalization of entrepreneurial spirit, supported by the privatization of the state-owned economy and the substantial increase of foreign investments. This Article focuses on the analysis of the emerging legal framework for entrepreneurship in Hungary that provides the basis for privatization and foreign investments.

II. Evolution of the Legal Framework for Entrepreneurship and Privatization in Hungary

Hungarian and other Eastern European commentators have neglected to provide proper legal analysis of the economic reform movement. The lack of a theoretical foundation for the fast-paced changes is a major contributing factor to this neglect. There is a consensus, however, on the point that nineteenth century Marxist ideology has not provided the necessary guidelines for running the state-controlled national economy. The economic reforms in Eastern Europe, particularly in Hungary, should be viewed as a continuous and frustrating search for effective solutions.

One of the fatal flaws to the post-Stalinist model in Hungary is the scope of authority of the State Property Agency to the enterprises and other assets operated by the local self-governments.[1]

The establishment of the State Property Agency, however, was not without its critics. A frequently raised misgiving concerning the creation of a new state institution to personify and represent social property was that the ownership interest of the society would not be realized more efficiently by bureaucratic "property ministry" than were realized earlier by the sectorial ministries. Limiting the

---

[1]*See* Act LXV of 1990 on Local Self-Governments, § 107(1)(6).

freedom of action of the supposedly much more prepared and skillful entrepreneurial motivated managers would mean a step backward in the direction of the administratively-owned and managed state economy that already was considered anti-quated. While the functioning of the State Property Agency slowed the course of spontaneous privatization, its aim was not to preserve, but rather to eliminate, ownership rights of the state in a transparent, con-trolled, and socially acceptable way.[2]

The State Property Agency is primarily a privatization agency rather than a superstructure or holding company for the management of state-owned enterprises. Its predominant role is to represent and ensure ownership interests of the state during the process of corporatization, restructuring, and divestiture. The agency obviously should not bring back the inefficient practice of administrative ownership of the previous era. Rather, it should serve as a small task force, not replacing the self-managing bodies of the state-owned enterprises, but only depriving them of crucial property rights that might create conflict of interest situations, or in the case of privatization, involve insider dealings.[3]

III. LEGAL SAFEGUARDS AND INCENTIVES FOR FOREIGN INVESTMENT IN HUNGARY

The new generation of leadership that has emerged in most Central and Eastern European states realizes the inefficiency of the formal, centrally planned economic structure. Consequently, Hungary instituted economic reforms that will enhance the social efficiency of production and allow more freedom for the supply and demand relations

---

[2]*See* Act VII, *supra* note 80 (preamble and legislative interpretation by the Minister of Justice).
[3]*Id.*

of market forces. One of the major objectives of these reforms was to integrate these economies into the world market by eliminating the artificial separation between the domestic and world market prices. The implementation of these changes laid the foundation of a more flexible, receptive system for the further expansion of these recent economic changes.[4]

The Central and Eastern European states constitute the third largest market area in the world. Although its growing rate has slowed in the course of the deepening economic crisis, there are opportunities that cannot be disregarded. In East-West trade, the basic objectives of the Western businessperson are to obtain optimal profit levels with minimum exposure to risk. The export-import trade and different forms of industrial cooperation provide economically feasible alternatives to reach these basic goals. Both of these alternatives, however, have well-known limitations essentially based on the lack of convertibility of the national currencies, the chronic shortage of hard currency reserves, and the escalating debt burden. Investment decisions imply a more complex, multi-dimensional list of goals and consequences. Undoubtedly, international legal safeguards as well as guarantees and incentives provided by the domestic legislation of the host country must be scrutinized closely.

A. International Legal Safeguards

The most reliable protection for foreign investors is offered by a network of international agreements. Hungary is a member of a large number of bilateral treaties protecting foreign investments, as well as multi-lateral conventions

---

[4]For an excellent discussion of the changing regulation of foreign trade in Central-Eastern Europe, see Naray, *The End of the Foreign Trade Monopoly (The Case of Hungary)*, 23 J. WORLD TRADE L. 85-97 (1989).

providing the same effect. For instance, Hungary has signed bilateral investment protection agreements with most of the members of the European Community.[5] Typically, these bilateral investment agreements provide for national as well as most favored nation treatment. These agreements particularly protect foreign investments from expropriation or other unreasonable state action by guaranteeing full and effective compensation in convertible currencies.

The legal protection of foreign investments also are manifest in the recently adopted Agreement Between the European Economic Community and the Hungarian Republic on Trade, Commercial and Economic Cooperation.[6] In addition, Hungary recently became a member of the World Bank Multilateral Investment Guarantee Agency (MIGA).[7] MIGA issues a variety of guarantees for the protection against loss arising from state actions and other non-commercial risks.

Although the governments of the United States and Hungary have been negotiating for an investment protection treaty, a wider range of bilateral treaties governing trading relations already are in force. Hungary was admitted to the General Agreement on Tariffs and Trade (GATT) in 1973, and

---

[5]As of March 1990, Hungary has signed bilateral investment protection treaties with the following states: Austria, Belgium, Luxemburg, Cyprus, Denmark, United Kingdom, Finland, France, Greece, Netherlands, Korean Republic, Federal Republic of Germany, Italy, Switzerland, and Sweden. *See* Kiraly, *The Opportunities and Limitations of the Hungarian Foreign Investment Code in the Increase of Foreign Investments,* 45 JOGTUDOMANYI, KOZLONY 144-49 (1990).

[6]*See* Agreement between the European Economic Community and the Hungarian People's Republic on Trade, Commercial and Economic Cooperation, 31 O.J. EUR. COMM. (No. L327) art. 2, at 3 (Nov. 30, 1988).

[7]Law Decree No. 7 of 1989 on the Promulgation of International Agreement on the Establishment of the International Investment Protection Agency (signed in Seoul on Oct. 11, 1985).

thereafter the United States and Hungary concluded an agreement on trade relations granting Hungary most favored nation treatment.[8] This non-discriminatory most favored nation treatment unfortunately was the subject of the Jackson-Vanik Amendment of the Trade Act of 1974.[9] Every year, the United States Congress monitored Hungarian performance of the basic human right of the freedom of movement and reported its finding to the President of the United States. This destabilized bilateral trading relations. Consequently, in 1988, Hungary adopted the first comprehensive legislation on immigration and emigration, guaranteeing the basic right of freedom of movement for all its citizens.[10] The United States Government then extended unconditional, permanent, most favored nation treatment for Hungary, placing trading relations on a long-term, stable, and non-discriminatory basis.

Recently, the United States and Hungary signed an agreement authorizing the access of protection by the Overseas Private Investment Corporation for American Investments in Hungary (OPIC).[11] OPIC is a United States agency that provides a wide range of insurance coverage for

---

[8]Agreement on Trade Relations Between the United States of America and the Hungarian People's Republic, Mar. 17, 1978, United States-Hungary, art. 1, 29 U.S.T. 2711, T.I.A.S. No. 8967.

[9]Trade Act of 1974, Pub. L. No. 93-618, 88 Stat. 1978 (1975) (codified as amended at 19 U.S.C. § 2101-2495 (1988)); see also Gabor, The Trade Act of 1974—Title IV: Considerations Involved in Granting Most Favored-Nation Status to the Nonmarket Economy Countries, 11 INT'L LAW. 517 (1977).

[10]Act XXIX of 1989 on Emigration and Immigration (Hung.), 71 Magyar Kozlony (Hungarian Official Gazette) 1200-04; see also Gabor, Reflections on the Freedom of Movement in Light of the Dismantled "Iron Curtain," 65 TUL. L. REV. 849, 855-61 (1991).

[11]Investment Guaranty Agreement between the Government of the Hungarian People's Republic and the Government of the United States of America, 74/1990 (Iv.25) Mtr. 36 Magyar Kozlony (Hungarian Official Gazette) 757-61 (Apr. 25, 1990).

non-commercial risks. OPIC's investment protection guarantees played a critical role in the steady increase of United States investments in the Hungarian economy during the last twelve months.

B. Foreign Investment Code: A Synopsis

Foreign investment is not a new phenomenon in Hungary. Shortly after the introduction of economic reform in 1968, Hungary adopted one of the first pieces of legislation addressing the establishment of joint ventures with foreign equity participation. The first Hungarian joint venture legislature enacted in 1972 is characterized by its limitations and shortcomings.[12] The legislation greatly curtailed the scope of joint venture activity and generally was restricted to production, commercial, and service activities. Tax incentives were missing, and the bureaucratic, time-consuming authorization process constituted a severe disincentive. This "half-hearted beginning" lasted until 1984 and 1985 when the tax rates on joint ventures were lowered by the government in an effort to stimulate the establishment of joint ventures.[13]

When economic reform received new emphasis in the late 1980s, interest in establishing joint ventures greatly increased. The authorization process was simplified and accelerated. The major breakthrough occurred in 1988 and 1989 when the "Velvet Revolution" lead to the first multi-party election in Hungary. Hungary adopted the Code of Economic Associations and, in conjunction, drafted a new Foreign Investment Code. The two Codes entered into force at the

---

[12]Decree No. 28/1972 (X.3) of the Minister of Finance on Economic Associations with Foreign Participation; *see also* Eichman, *Joint Ventures in Hungary: A Model for Socialist States,* 20 LAW & POL'Y INT'L BUS. 257-62 (1988).

[13]*See* Eichman, *supra* note 101, at 260.

same time on January 1, 1989.[14]

Act XXIV of 1988 on Foreign Investment in Hungary (Investment Code or Code) is one of the most comprehensive pieces of Hungarian legislation designed to protect foreign investments.   Selected provisions of the Code recently were amended by Act XCVIII, which entered into force on January 1, 1991.[15] The Investment Code will play a major role in the transformation of the Hungarian economy to a free market economy system.   This objective of the Code is inseparable from the accompanying Act on Business Associations, which provides a list of organizational forms for foreign investors. The movement of privatization is also inseparable from the full understanding and the implementation of the Code.   Clearly, only foreign investors will have the substantial working capital resources necessary to take the major steps toward privatization within a national economy that is still seventy to eighty percent state-owned.

1.   Analysis of State Guarantees on the Level of the Act of Parliament

The Code basically follows two interrelated approaches. The first approach sets out a clear framework of safeguards for foreign investors.   The second approach elaborates on a wide range of incentives to attract foreign investment into the Hungarian national economy.

Although the "Cold War" is over, bad memories of arbitrary state actions by past communist regimes still linger in the minds of potential foreign investors.   Therefore, article 1 of the Investment Code states emphatically that "[i]nvestments of Foreign Investors in Hungary shall enjoy full protection and

---

[14]*See supra* note 68.

[15]Act XCVIII of 1990 Amendment of the Act XXIV of 1988 on Foreign Investment in Hungary, 137 Magyar Kozlony (Hungarian Official Gazette) 2746-49 (Dec. 29, 1990).

security."[16] This fundamental safeguard is implemented by the commitment of full and immediate compensation by the state administrative agencies involved in nationalization, expropriation, or other measures having an equivalent effect on the ownership right of a foreign investor. The Code also provides that the actions of the state administrative agency are subject to judicial review.[17]

Finally, the Code provides that compensation shall be in the currency in which the investment took place. Article 13 of the 1989 constitutional amendment elevated this basic right of ownership to a constitutional guarantee providing that "property can only be taken by exception and for public purpose in the defined cases of the law accompanied by full, unconditional and immediate compensation."[18] The constitutional amendment does not draw a distinction between Hungarian and foreign owned property. In this respect, Hungary clearly is in full compliance with its international treaty obligations, as well as the general principles of customary international law. Today, the quest for privatization and reprivatization is on the national agenda and the sanctity of foreign-owned property is fully safeguarded

---

[16] *Id.* art. 1.

[17] *See* Act XXIV of 1988 on Foreign Investment in Hungary, *supra* note 68, art. 1 (Jan. 1, 1989), translated in Hungaro Press at 1 (Apr. 1990), which provides:
  1) Investments of foreign investors in Hungary shall enjoy full protection and security.
  2) All loses [sic] suffered by a foreign investor due to nationalization, expropriation, or other measures having equivalent effect on ownership rights, shall be compensated at real value without delay.
  3) Such compensation shall be made by the state administrative organ that has taken the measure in question. In case of infringement of law, review of the state administrative organ's action can be requested from the court.
  4) The compensation shall be paid to the person entitled thereto in the currency in which his investment took place.

[18] *See* Act XXXI, *supra* note 56, § 13.

in Hungary.

2.   Forms of Foreign Participation in Hungarian Economic
Associations

The organizational alternatives of foreign investors are
regulated by Act VI of 1988 on Economic Associations, which
entered into force in conjunction with the Investment Code.[19]
In this respect, foreign natural and legal persons can invest in
an   economic   association   presently   having   foreign
participation, establish a new economic association with
foreign participation, or make investments in a Hungarian
Economic Association.   Foreign investors prefer two basic
organizational forms. Small or medium size operations prefer
the limited liability company model, while larger scale
operations generally choose the company limited by shares
forms.   A careful cost-benefit analysis should precede the
selection of the appropriate organizational form.   In addition,
the Code provides that foreign investors can pursue any
economic activity except as prohibited or limited by law.[20]
The   original   act   does   not   require   governmental
authorization for the operation of foreign investors if their
capital contribution does not exceed forty-nine percent. If the
majority ownership is in the hands of foreign investors, joint
permission from the Minister of Finance and the Minister of
Trade is required. Permission must be granted within ninety
days   from   the   date   of   filing,   otherwise   permission   is
considered granted.[21] This provision clearly indicates the
flexibility and the relaxation of the bureaucratic restrictions on
the authorization process. The new amendment to article 1
completely eliminated even this governmental authorization

---

[19] *See supra* note 66.
[20] *See* Act XXIV of 1988, *supra* note 104, § 9(1).
[21] *Id.* § 8(1).

requirement, stating "the foundation of an Association with foreign capital does not require any permission from the foreign exchange or other governmental authorities."[22] This means that the newly established company must be recorded only in the court of registry, which has a limited function of legal assessment and legal supervision for the Authority is not necessary to the establishment of an Association operating with foreign malities of the establishment of the business organization.

3.   Property Ownership

The Investment Code emphasizes the implementation of the "national treatment" principle.   This principle is particularly relevant in guaranteeing the unconditional right of acquisition of real property for the operation of the company with foreign participation. Until recently, a joint venture could acquire Hungarian real property only with the permission of the Minister of Finance. Now, article XIX of the Code provides the basic right to acquire ownership of real property necessary for the economic activities of the association with foreign participation.[23] This provision is fully consistent with the national treatment principle and offers significant incentives for the foreign investor.[24]At the same time, the provision is

---

[22]*See* act XCVIII of 1990, *supra* note 104, § 1(2). The permission of the Foreign Exchange Authority is not necessary to the establishment of an Association operating with foreign participation.

[23]*See* Act XXIV of 1988 on foreign Investment in Hungary, *supra* note 69, art. 19 (Jan. 1, 1989), translated in Hungaro Press at 6 (Apr. 1990), which provides:

The Association:

a) May acquire ownership or other real estate rights necessary for its economic activity as defined in the Contract of Association; and

b) may manage all of its assets in accordance with Hungarian law and the provisions of the Contract of Association.

[24]*See supra* note 104. Act XXIV of 1988 at § 19 and

based on the implementation of the Hungarian Code on Private International Law, which provides that the "legal capacity, economic qualification, personal legal rights, and membership relations of the legal person shall be governed by its personal law. . . . The personal law of a legal person is the law of the state, in whose territory the legal person was taken into registry."[25] Thus, if the company with foreign participation is registered in the Hungarian court, it must be treated as a Hungarian company under Hungarian private international law as well as under general international law principles. Thus, these investors are entitled to the economic and legal capacity necessary to fulfill their economic function, including the acquisition of real property.

---

accompanying legislative interpretation.

[25] *See* Law Decree No. 13 of 1979 on Private International Law of the President's Council of the Hungarian People's Republic, 33 Magyar Kozlong (Hungarian Official Gazette) 495-514. Section 18 provides:

Legal Persons

§ 18 [1] The legal capacity, economic qualification, personal legal rights and membership relations of the legal person shall be governed by its personal law.

[2] The personal law of a legal person is the law of the State, in whose territory the legal person was taken into registry.

[3] If the legal person is registered according to the law of several states, or registration is not necessary according to the controlling law of its seat, its personal law is the controlling law of its seat designated in its charter.

[4] If the legal person has no seat according to its charter, or it has several seats, which were not registered under the laws of either state, its personal law is the law of the State, where the central management is located.

[5] The personal law of the separately registered branch or plant of a legal person is the law of the State where the branch or plant was registered.

See also Gabor, *A Socialist Approach to Codification of Private International Law in Hungary: Comments and Translation,* 55 TUL. L. REV. 63 (1980).

4.   Tax Allowances and Incentives

In January 1989, Hungary introduced a single unified tax system into the economy. The Code emphasizes that this unified tax system applies to companies operating with foreign participation. The controlling principle of national treatment is that these companies pay exactly the same amount of tax as domestic enterprises. The Code also emphasizes that the entrepreneurship tax is the only tax that must be paid to Hungary's Treasury.

At the same time, the Code provides a package of tax incentives and benefits that provides significantly better tax treatment for foreign-controlled companies as compared with domestic counterparts. The amended Code focuses on the activities and the amount of investment in the association as the basis of scale for the tax benefits. Article IV of the recent amendment provides that if more than half the earnings of the enterprise are derived from production or the operation of a hotel, and the invested capital exceeds fifty million forints (approximately eight million dollars), and the foreign participation is at least thirty percent, then the company is entitled to a sixty percent tax reduction for its first five years and a forty percent deduction from the sixth until the tenth year.[26]

The amended Code extended the list of economic activities of significant importance to the Hungarian national economy, including the production of electronic and vehicle components packaging technology, telecommunications, and the tourist industry.[27] For these highly value activities, the

---

[26] See Act XCVIII of 1990, *supra* note 104, § 4(2)(6).

[27] The appendix to art. 15, para. 2, subpara. c of Act XXIV of 1988 provides: ACTIVITIES OF OUTSTANDING IMPORTANCE TO THE HUNGARY ECONOMY

1. Electronics:
    a) production   of   active,   passive   and   electro-mechanic

components;

b) production of computer (hardware) peripherals;

c) production of electronically controlled telecommunication main and subcenters;

d) production of instruments for robotics and services relating thereto;

e) production of computer-aided design (CAD) systems; and

f) production of electronical equipment, including electronical products for every-day use.

2. Production of vehicle components.

3. Production of machinery.

4. Production of machinery and equipment for agriculture, food, industry and forestry.

5. Engineering Units:

a) production of high precision cast, wrought or press-forged components and pre-fabricated elements;

b)production of components and spare parts of general use (quality fittings, valves, hydraulic and pneumatic components, advanced anti-friction bearings and spare parts, high- strain resistant artificial material parts, technological constituents);

a) production of up-to-date joining fittings;

b) production of tools and appliances; and production of technical ceramics.

6. Packaging technology:

a) production of package material and equipment; and

b) production of package machines.

7. Production of pharmaceuticals, plant-protecting agents and intermediers [sic]:

a) production of new pharmaceuticals;

b) production of new plant-protecting agents;

c) production of key-intermediaries for pharmaceuticals & plant-protecting agents; and

d) production of veterinary preparations.

8. Manufacture of products for agriculture and food developed for increase of exports and the decrease of imports effected in freely convertible currency.

9. Development of home protein stock.

10. Production of propagation and breeding material.

11. Field of materials and energy conservation:

a) manufacture of products developed by a technology enabling the creation of smaller bulk and more up-to-date constructions (e.g., high-tensile component materials, high-grade clean materials, material-improving technologies);

b) production of units used for the permanent control and measurement of the qualitative parameters of technological specifications applied in process control;

amended Code provides that if the amount of foreign investment exceeds fifty million forints and the percentage of the foreign investment is at least thirty percent, then the company is entitled to a one hundred percent tax exemption for the first five years of operation and a sixty percent allowance from the sixth year to the tenth year, which can be used in the form of retention of the tax.[28] Additional tax exemptions guarantee the retention of tax for the reinvestment of the earned profits, thereby stimulating reinvestment. Finally, in the case of investments made by the association, one hundred percent of the value added tax in the relevant fiscal year as previously determined may be retained from the tax payment.

From the outset, the legislative purpose of the amended Code is to stimulate foreign investments in those areas of the

---

c) production of instruments for technologies concerning the improvement of the economy of waste profiles; and
d) production of equipment for the economic utilization of big bulk by-products and waste material (e.g., in forestry, plant cultivation, stock breeding).
12. Telecommunications.
13. Tourism:
a) establishment and catering of establishments of thermal and medicinal baths if run by the investor;
b) reconstruction of manor houses declared historic buildings; and
c) establishment and catering of medium class hotel chains if run by the investors.
14. Manufacturing of products developed on the basis of bio-technic or biotechnology.
Id. See supra note 100, § 12 Amendments:
15. Public Transportation Vehicles
16. Motorcycles, MOPED
17. Personal automobile
18. Autobus
19. Gasoline operated truck
20. Diesel truck
21. Dump truck
22. Special purpose public road vehicle.
[28] See Act XCVIII of 1990, supra note 104, § 4.

national economy in which technological improvements and the injection of working capital are most critical, as well as to encourage the inflow of working capital on a larger scale.

5.   Duty Free Imports and the Transfer of Profits

The accelerated improvement of technological and technical conditions is the major economic and political purpose of the amended Code. Therefore, the foreign investor will have to contribute cash in a freely convertible currency. The means of production and equipment for permanent use can be contributed in kind to the association by its foreign member and may be imported into the state, free of duty. The Code also specifies that if the association sells the imported means of production or leases it within a three year period, the duty must be paid subsequently.[29]

One of the major concerns of foreign investors is the repatriation of the profits in convertible currencies. While the Hungarian Government has been making serious efforts to make its national currency convertible by 1992, it is not completely convertible at the present time. Even the Hungarian National Bank sets the exchange rates realistically and has allowed the forints to float against the basket of Western currencies since 1981. The discrepancy between the official rate and the black market rate generally does not exceed ten to fifteen percent. Under these conditions, the most significant safeguard provided in article 32 of the Code guarantees that:

> The amount due to the foreign party from an Association's profits, the amount due to the foreign party in case of the Association's dissolution or in case of total or partial alienation or transfer of his share can, provided that the

---

[29]*Id.* § 5.

Association possesses the amount due in Forint, be freely transferred abroad in the currency of the investment under the instructions of the foreign party.[30]

The Hungarian National Bank, following the current official exchange rate, transfers the earned profits in the convertible currencies of the investors.

It is a noteworthy incentive that foreign-controlled associations are exempted from complying with some labor law regulations. In Hungary, most wages are government-controlled. The association is exempt from wage regulations if foreign participation exceeds twenty percent. This is important as far as wage regulation incentives relate to the composition of the leading officials of the association. At the same time, fifty percent of the taxed personal income of the foreign managerial employees can be fully transferred into the currency of the state in which they are permanent residents.

6.   Companies in Custom Free Zones

An association with foreign participation can be established in custom free zones, which allow treatment as foreign territory from the perspective of the application of custom laws and procedures, foreign exchange rules, banking regulations, and other state regulatory controls. The foreign association operating in custom free zones is treated as a foreign company. Its accounting systems are in fully convertible currencies, and it conducts foreign trade activities, such as commodities, with those states with which Hungary currently has international treaties specifying the kind and quantity of commodities to be exported or imported.[31]

---

[30] *See* Act XXIV of 1988, *supra* note 69, § 32.
[31] *Id.* §§ 37-39.

7.   Private International Law Safeguards

International and domestic safeguards and guarantees cannot offer complete security for the private contracting parties. It is important, therefore, to plan for legal disputes in the construction and the performance of the foreign investment. Article 44 of the Code provides that legal disputes of the association can be settled by domestic or foreign ordinary courts or by arbitration tribunal, provided that the parties stipulate in advance and in writing the place and the manner of the dispute settlements.

Generally, the Western party probably will be reluctant to submit to the jurisdiction of the ordinary court in Hungary. Arbitration tribunals attached to the Hungarian Chamber of Commerce can provide a more expert and objective treatment of investment disputes. Probably the most favorable solution, from the standpoint of the Western investor, is to stipulate the arbitration forum in its own jurisdiction or in a well-recognized neutral third forum. Hungary, as well as the United States and most of the OECD states, is a member of 1958 Convention for the Recognition and Enforcement of Foreign Arbitration Awards. This provides basic assurances that the Hungarian parties as well as the foreign party will submit to arbitration and the resulting award will receive full recognition and enforcement.

As far as choice of law is concerned, the Hungarian Code on Private International Law provides basic guidelines. Undoubtedly, most of the provisions of the Foreign Investment Code as well as the relevant part of, the Code on Business Associations relating to the organization and the functioning of companies limited by shares are mandatory in their character. Thus, the parties do not enjoy the choice of law freedom to stipulate or avoid the binding effect of this law. On the other hand, the limited liability company and different general and limited partnership forms mostly contain dispositive type rules in which the parties' choice of law freedom can be exercised.

It is also important to emphasize that the legal background for any foreign operation is found in the Hungarian Civil Code, and most of its operative provisions provide dispositive types of rules. Article 36 of the Foreign Investment Code specifically exempts the foreign participation association from the widespread state regulatory framework that only affects state-owned enterprises and cooperative organizations. Therefore, the parties in a foreign association should scrutinize closely the limitations imposed on the Hungarian legal system and exercise their contractual choice of law freedom that is permissible under the Hungarian legal system.[32]

IV. Conclusion: Economic Transformation from the Human Perspective

Hungary is struggling in its economic transformation into a free market economic system. The economic reform movement in the last twenty-three years set the foundation for this process. Now, the people are enjoying political freedom after forty years of domination and demand an effective course of action for economic transformation. At the same time, Hungary is experiencing the highest per capita debt in the region, thirty-five to forty percent rate of inflation, and a fast rising rate of unemployment, all of which have placed an intolerable burden on a population unaccustomed to the symptoms of an economic crisis during forty-five years of communist stagnation. The tolerance level and expectations

---

[32] See Gabor, *Private International Law Aspects of East-West Trade: Synopsis of Recent Developments*, 16 INT'L J. LEGAL INFO. 3 (1988).

of the people will demand close scrutinization.

The creative entrepreneurial spirit of the people has to be rediscovered and stimulated by providing a legal framework for entrepreneurial activities. In this respect, the legalization of the second economy in the early 1980s and the creation of a more stable framework for business activities in the late 1980s can be considered positive signs of development.

The critical issue now is the privatization of the tremendous state-owned sector, which includes seventy-five to eighty percent of the national economy. Economic resources of the population are limited, and the people lack interest in taking over a relatively inefficient state-owned sector. The only realistic hope, therefore, lies in the effective stimulation of the inflow of foreign working capital.[33] Hopefully, the new Act on Company Law, in conjunction with the Foreign Investment Code as recently amended, will provide a solid legal basis for this process.

---

[33] See, e.g., O. HIERONYMI, HUNGARIAN ECONOMIC, FINANCIAL AND MONCLAIR POLICIES: PROPOSALS FOR A COHERENT APPROACH (1990).

2. Reflections on NATO's New Mission: Conflict Prevention in the Struggles for Ethnic Self-Determination

29 REV. CEN. & E. EUR. L. 247 (2004)

*Reprinted with permission, Koninklijke Brill N.V.
Printed in The Netherlands*

FRANCIS A. GABOR[*]

Abstract

During the Cold War, both NATO's role and purpose were clearly defined by the existence of the threat posed by the Soviet Union. The traditional confrontation between the NATO and the Warsaw Pact military organizations effectively has ceased to exist. The dissolution of the Warsaw Pact—combined with the emerging constitutional democracies in Central and Eastern Europe and the transformation of the Russian Federation—has essentially assured that the future threat of a confrontation between the major armies on the European continent is highly unlikely. However, it soon became obvious that several non-traditional, and quite unexpected, risks would give NATO a new mission and new challenges.

One of the greatest challenges for post. Cold War Eastern Europe lies in the unresolved questions of ethnic self-determination. The unprecedented human tragedy of two world wars failed to resolve these questions. The concept of

---

[*] The writing of this Article was supported by a research grant provided by the University of Memphis Cecil C. Humphreys School of Law. The author wishes to express his appreciation to Kristy Gunn, a recent graduate of the University of Memphis, for her assistance in the writing of this article.

123

ethnic self-determination has been the central theme of the conflicts in the Yugoslav civil wars. NATO played a significant, if not central, role in the final resolution of the Yugoslav civil wars, particularly in the case of Kosovo. The Kosovo experience creates a real challenge for NATO and international legal scholars to create a more precisely defined body of international law to protect ethnic minorities and to build an effective institutional framework for the observation and implementation of so-called minority rights which would have prevented the tragedy of the Yugoslavian civil war and can prevent future conflicts.

1. Historical Reflections

The world order has changed in fundamental ways since the creation of both NATO and the United Nations. The end of the Cold War, in the early 1990s has necessitated a re-evaluation of the role of the North American Treaty Organization (NATO) as a defense mechanism and of the role of the United Nations in its pursuit of peace and stability throughout the world. The lines between the roles of these two organizations and their authority have become, to some extent, blurred. The experience in Kosovo highlights the modern problems of ethnic self-determination and peaceful nation building. Which organization is most equipped to conduct humanitarian interventions both military and non-military, and which is most equipped to build a nation when the immediate problems that necessitated the intervention have been solved? The military action in Iraq that erupted in March 2003 raised these questions and begs reflection on the circumstances that created the current world order and on the lessons that can be learned there from.

The unprecedented devastation of the two world wars has been one of the hallmarks of twentieth century history. It

124

would be interesting to travel back in an imaginary time machine and establish NATO at the conclusion of the 1907 Peace Conferences at The Hague. What would be the impact of this hypothetical assumption? The threshold Article 5 of the NATO Treaty would extend collective self-defense for all the member states.[1] The pivotal question in this hypothetical is whether Germany and its allies would have joined this convention. Historical reality reveals that mutual defense treaties and organizations are always established against common enemies.

All the European powers, including Germany, ratified the General Treaty for the Renunciation of War (Kellogg-Briand Pact) in 1928; however, the rising axis powers soon disregarded its application.[2] Thus, the lack of a mutual defense treaty system and the weak conflict prevention machinery of the League of Nations led to the most devastating destruction in human history: the loss of fifty-five million human lives in the Second World War.[3]

From the ashes of the most devastating human tragedy, a new international legal order emerged in 1945. The United Nations was created to preserve peace and security and to prevent the reoccurrence of war, Article 2, Paragraph 4 of the United Nations Charter[4] proclaims the use of force, or the threat of its use, to be illegal and pronounces it to be a

---

[1]North Atlantic Treaty (NATO Treaty), 63 Stat. 2241,T.I.A.S. No. 1964; 34 UNT.S. 243., signed at Washington on 4 April 1949; entered into force on 24 August 1949; Art.V.

[2]46 Stat. 2343, 94 L.N.T.S. 57. The Kellogg—Briand Pact became effective on 24 July 1929 and it is still in force.

[3]C. Brölman et al. (eds.), *Peoples and Minorities in International Law*, Dordrecht 1996, 86.

[4]Charter of the United Nations signed in San Francisco, 26 June 1945. On the viability of Article 2(4), see L. Henkin, *How Nations Behave* 146-53 (2d ed. 1978); O. Schachter, *In Defense of International Rules on the Use of Force*, 53 U. Chi. L. Rev. 1986, 113.

violation of a peremptory norm of general international law.[5] The Security Council was established for the implementation of this fundamental principle in pursuit of the United Nation's ultimate goal: the preservation of peace and security throughout the globe. Under Chapter VII of the United Nations Charter, the victorious allied powers represented by the United States, the United Kingdom, France, the Soviet Union, and China became the permanent members of the Security Council. Any enforcement action with respect to threats to the peace, breaches of the peace, and acts of aggression require the unanimous consent of these five nations.

For a brief time, mankind's dream of creating a world government assuring peace and security on our planet seemed to becoming a reality. Unfortunately, the Cold War frustrated the high expectations for a world government. For some forty years, the United Nations Organization and its activities were hampered and often thwarted by the Cold War. The Security Council was largely incapacitated in its principal role of maintaining international peace and security by lack of agreement (and by veto) of the permanent members.[6]

The Soviet Union did not live up to its "Gentleman's Agreement" from Yalta: the commitment to free elections for the peoples of Central and Eastern Europe was denied, and communist-controlled governments were imposed on them. By 1949, an "Iron Curtain" had fallen upon the countries of Central and Eastern Europe, and the dangerous East-West

---

[5]See generally Louis B. Sohn, "How American International Lawyers Prepared for the San Francisco Bill of Rights", 89 AM. J. INT'L L. 540–53 (1995).

[6]Henkin, op.cit., 112–18; see, also, B. Asrat, Prohibition of Force under the UN Charter :A Study of Article 2 (4), Stockholm 1991, 69-94.

confrontation of the Cold War began its forty-year evolution.[7]

2. International Legal Framework of NATO

The Soviet threat intensified in 1948 when Moscow imposed a land blockade on Berlin but it refrained from threatening the Western enclaves or hampering the airlift. Containment of the Soviet expansion became the primary foreign policy objective of the United States and the war-torn nations of Western Europe. Historically, NATO emerged in large part as a response to the security threats coming from the Soviet Union and the Eastern Bloc, simultaneously providing the cement to bind former WWII adversaries into a unified security structure.[8] The twelve original members signed the NATO treaty in Washington on 4 April 1949 with the goal of providing a collective defense for the preservation of peace and security in the North Atlantic region.[9]

This collective self-defense system is based on Article 51 of the United Nations Charter and Article 5 of the Washington Treaty which envisages that an armed attack against one or more of the parties to the Treaty shall be considered an attack against all.[10] Consequently, in case of such an armed attack, members are compelled to assist the attacked party by taking individually or in concert with other parties such action as each deems necessary, including the use of armed force, to restore and maintain the security of the North Atlantic area. Today NATO member states are: Belgium, Canada, Denmark, France, Germany, Greece, Iceland, Italy, Luxembourg, The Netherlands, Norway, Portugal, Spain, Turkey, the United Kingdom, and the United States, and—

---

[7]Id.

[8]S. Trifunovska, *The Transatlantic Alliance on the Eve of the New Millennium,* Leiden 1996, 7-14.

[9]NATO Treaty Preamble.

[10]NATO Treaty Art.V.

after the 1999 enlargement—Hungary, Poland, and the Czech Republic.

The North Atlantic Treaty clearly recognizes the supremacy of the United Nations Charter and its preeminent role as the authority in the resolution of international disputes.[11] The threshold Article V of the North Atlantic Treaty refers to the right of individual and collective self-defense recognized by Article 51 of the Charter of the United Nations "consistent with the authority of the Security Council (Art. V)". The principal articles of the Treaty clearly suggest that the alliance acts under the guidelines of the UN Charter and strictly adheres to its Purposes and Principles. However, the Treaty members assert that NATO is not a regional organization under Chapter VIII of the Charter; instead, they insist that NATO was created solely under the auspices of Article 51 of the Charter and, therefore, is a collective self-defense organization only.[12]

Despite the disclaimer language in Article V of the Treaty, NATO has not restricted itself to collective self-defense actions. Taking on the tasks typical of a regional organization, NATO's boundaries have been extended to promote economic and scientific cooperation, in addition to its strictly military purposes. During the Yugoslav civil wars, NATO played a vital role in peacekeeping actions.[13] Thus, NATO also fulfills the

---

[11]NATO Treaty Art.I.

[12]See *supra* note 8, at 19–20.

[13]General Framework Agreement for Peace in Bosnia and Herzegovina, UN Doc S/1995/999 (1995), which was initialed at Dayton and formally signed at Paris on 14 December 1995. *See* 35 I.L.M. 75 (1996). It was approved by the Security Council and placed on a Chapter VII footing in Resolution 1033 (15 December 1995). The Dayton Agreement replaced UNPROFOR with a new force under NATO auspices, known as the Implementation Force or IFOR. IFOR was both substantially larger (up to 60,000 troops) and more robust in its mandate than UNPROFOR. In a slightly scaled-down version known as the Stability Force (SFOR), the NATO force has

functions of a regional organization, but it will, of course, be free from Security Council involvement as long as its actions are justifiable under the Charter's Article 51 provision for individual and collective self-defense. However, when engaged in policies other than collective self-defense actions designed to promote peace and security, NATO will be subject to the notification and approval requirements found in Chapter VIII, as would any other organization.[14]

During the Cold War, both NATO's role and purpose were clearly defined by the existence of the threat posed by the Soviet Union. No doubt the widening technological superiority enjoyed by NATO over the Warsaw Pact states played a major role in the winning of the Cold War by the West. By the early 1990's, the Warsaw Pact had been dissolved at the insistence of the newly liberated countries of Central and Eastern Europe, and the Soviet Union had collapsed. With the end of the Cold War, a unique opportunity has arisen to construct a new, group-security architecture in the whole of the Euro-Atlantic Area. The aim of this new architecture has been to provide increased stability and security for all nations in the Euro-Atlantic area without creating dividing lines. NATO views security as a broad concept embracing political and economic as well as defense components. In this process of concerted stabilization, the Alliance has played—and will play—a strong and essential role in preserving stability and

---

remained in Bosnia-Herzegovina and is still in place as of early 2001. *See generally* S. Murphy, *Humanitarian Intervention: The United Nations in an Evolving World Order,* Philadelphia 1996, 198-217; R. Ullman (ed.), *The World and Yugoslavia's Wars,* New York 1996, on the negotiations for the Dayton Agreement; see H. Holbrooke, *To End a War,* NewYork 1998, for references on the Kosovo conflict.

[14]Jeffrey Palmer, "The New European Order: Restructuring the Security Regime under the Conference on Security and Cooperation in Europe", 5 TEMP. INT'L & COMP. L. J. 1991, 66-72.

security in Europe.[15]

3. New Mission of the NATO Conflict Prevention and Management in the Struggles for Ethnic Self-Determination

The traditional confrontation between the NATO and the Warsaw Pact military organizations effectively has ceased to exist. The dissolution of the Warsaw Pact—combined with the emerging constitutional democracies in Central and Eastern Europe and the transformation of the Russian Federation—has essentially assured that the future threat of a confrontation between the major armies on the European continent is highly unlikely. Skeptical voices argued that with this transformation in the post-Cold War environment, the principal reason for the existence of the NATO alliance has also ceased to exist and, therefore, that NATO should abandon its mission. These skeptical voices from both sides of the Atlantic could not appreciate the fast-pace of events following 1989. However, it soon became obvious that several non-traditional, and quite unexpected, risks would give NATO a new mission and new challenges.[16]

One of the greatest challenges for post-Cold War Eastern Europe lies in the unresolved questions of ethnic self-determination. The unprecedented human tragedy of two world wars failed to resolve these questions. The Marxist dominated regimes in Central and Eastern Europe made extraordinary efforts to ignore and oppress any open debate on the question of ethnic self-determination.[17] The turning

---

[15]Rob de Wijk, *NATO on the Brink of the New Millennium* 23-31 (London 1998).

[16]Jane Meyer, *Collective Self-Defense and Regional Security: Necessary Exceptions to a Globalist Doctrine II*, B.U. INT'L L. J., 1993, 394-401.

[17]Brölman *et al., op. cit.*, 3–27.

130

point came with the unexpectedly fast collapse of communist control as "the Velvet Revolution" swept across the region in 1988 and 1990. However, the astonishing pace of political transformation was not accompanied by a balanced economic transition to free market economies.[18] Most of the countries of Central and Eastern Europe have been undergoing unprecedented economic crises.[19] Furthermore, ethnic conflict has reemerged as the political central authority has been weakened by the ongoing economic crises.[20]

After 1989, the sudden collapse of both the external and internal Marxist central authorities created a dangerous power vacuum in the Central and East European region. The struggle for ethnic self-determination became the dominant ideological force in the course of the disintegration of the Soviet Union and, in particular, Yugoslavia. The Yugoslav tragedy offers a particularly compelling case for a new approach to the different levels of self-determination in the post-Cold War period. In Yugoslavia, it became quite obvious that territorial integrity and ethnic self-determination could not be peacefully reconciled in the midst of the collapse of the central political and economic authorities. The struggle for ethnic self-determination led to genocide and "ethnic cleansing". People retracted into their tribal state, trying to destroy historical human realities.[21] Thus, the vague notion of ethnic self-determination had become a destructive force.

From a historical perspective, the ethnic conflicts in Central and Eastern Europe are merely the continuation of unresolved questions in international law: how to protect

---

[18]Anne Orford, *Locating the International: Military and Monetary Intervention after the Cold War*, 38 HARV. INT'L L. J. 1997, 443-447.

[19]*See supra* note 20, at 29–25.

[20]*Id.* at 29–35.

[21]*Id.* at 21–27.

ethnic minorities residing in the territory of another sovereign nation-state where the borders of nation-states do not necessarily follow the historical settlement of ethnic populations? After each world war, people and national borders were artificially rearranged, disregarding any effective protection of ethnic minorities.[22] Therefore, it is not surprising that the issues of ethnic self-determination remain to be addressed by the global community of nations in the post-Cold War era.

The concept of ethnic self-determination has been the central theme of the conflicts in the Yugoslav civil wars. NATO played a significant, if not central, role in the final resolution of the Yugoslav civil wars, particularly in the case of Kosovo. Having said this, the traditional role and experience of the NATO did not well prepare it well for conflict prevention and management of the unprecedented dimension presented by the Yugoslav civil wars. At the end game in Kosovo, while the European Union and the Organization for Security and Cooperation in Europe attempted to play a political role in the mediation and conflict prevention, the process eventually demanded the use of real force by NATO. After the experience in Bosnia with the United Nations peacekeeping forces and the paralyzed deployment of NATO forces during that course of events, the survival of NATO seemed to be at stake and to be intimately connected with the issue of resorting peace and security in the Kosovo province. Faced with the prospect of massive genocide and the brutal acts of the Yugoslav army, the security forces in the international community were forced to act. The process in Ramboulier produced a political document reflecting a compromise that was not accepted by the Yugoslav government, leaving the use of NATO forces as

---

[22]*Id.* at 77–101.

the only alternative to implement the Ramboulier Accord.[23]

The founding treaty of NATO requires that NATO act in a manner consistent with the fundamental mandates and principles of the UN Charter. Specifically, any Chapter VII enforcement action requires the authorization of the Security Council, but it was a well calculated prediction that two of the permanent members—Russia and China—would not consent to such action and, thus, would veto any resolution to deploy NATO forces. Therefore, the United Nations Security Council did not approve a resolution authorizing the deployment of NATO forces until after the use of such forces led to the adoption of the Ramboulier Accord. International scholars argue that this case should not be construed as a precedent for grand scale avoidance of both Security Council authorization and the fundamental principles expressed in the United Nations Charter. Rather, this event should be viewed as an isolated action justified either under traditional customary international law as a humanitarian intervention preventing genocide or as an international legal necessity to intervene and protect humanity.[24]

The pertinent question is: What lesson can be learned from the Kosovo experience for the future of NATO in conflict prevention of the same nature? The Kosovo experience creates a real challenge for NATO and international legal scholars to create a more precisely defined body of international law to protect ethnic minorities and build an effective institutional framework for the observation and implementation of so-called minority rights.[25] Perhaps the existence of such a system

---

[23]Francis A. Gabor, *An International Legal Perspective on Ethnic Self-Determination in Central-Eastern Europe*, 5 PARKER SCH. J. OF E. EUR. L. 498–99 (1998).

[24]L. Henkin, *Kosovo and the Law of 'Humanitarian Intervention*, 93 AM. J. INT'L L. 824–28 (1999).

[25]David M. Kresock, *Ethnic Cleansing in the Balkans: A Legal*

would have prevented the tragedy of the Yugoslavian civil war that led to ethnic cleansing, genocide, and other atrocious crimes against humanity by resolving a problem not properly treated or addressed under the current body of international law.

Clearly, the people in Bosnia-Herzegovina, as well as in Kosovo, had no faith in the ability of public international law to protect their minority rights for the preservation of their national culture, language, and other basic phenomena of existence.[26] The end of the Kosovo tragedy will lead to the acceleration of the expansion of the European Union to the Southeastern European Region. The economic and political integration of the European Union has manifested in the emerging supranational decision-making, which necessarily limits the sovereignty of the member states. Ethnic-religious-linguistic minorities have been receiving wide-scale recognition and protection in the emerging body of European minority rights.[27] An institutional framework has also developed for the effective protection and implementation of these rights.[28]

In the light of the Kosovo conflict, new norms of customary international law have emerged, promoting the crystallization of rules for international self-determination of peoples of a sovereign state.[29] Traditionally, the international

---

Foundation of Foreign Intervention, 27 CORNELL INT'L L. J. 203 (1994).

[26]*Id.* at 208.

[27]D. Wippman, International Law and Ethnic Conflict, Ithaca 1998, 2–21.

[28]*Id.* at 7–18.

[29]Gareth Evans, "The Responsibility to Protect", *NATO Review,* Winter Issue 2002, *available at* http://www.nato.int/docu/review/2002/issue4/english/ analysis.html. (explaining the findings of the International Commission on Intervention and State Sovereignty established by Canada in 2002). The Commission determined that a new international norm was emerging: the "responsibility to protect" to all peoples. *Id.* This responsibility to protect is primarily in the

community expressed a very cautious approach in recognizing internal self-determination of ethnic minorities living within the boundaries of a sovereign nation-state.[30] It is evident that the political underpinning of this position is the fear that minorities, by invoking claims of rights to self-determination, might then claim a right of secession. This fear exists because self-determination still means statehood to many.[31] In fact, in

---

hands of the nation concerned, but when a state fails to honor this obligation the international community must act in its stead. *Id.* The Commission further found that this responsibility to protect included the need to react, prevent, and rebuild. *Id.; see generally* Reference in Re Secession of Quebec, 2 S.C.R. 217 (Can. 1998) (asserting that international law recognizes the right of self-determination by peoples but with limitations).

[30]Ian Brownlie, "The Rights of Peoples in Modern International Law", in James Crawford (ed.), *The Rights of Peoples,* Oxford 1988, 5.

[31]One political consequence of the prospective expansion of the European Union has been the tenuous agreement between Romania and Hungary not to revive their ancient quarrel over Transylvania. *See* Garret Fitzgerald, "What is so different about being European?" *Irish Times,* 25 January 2003. Recently, however, this tenuous peace has been disrupted by repeated assertions of autonomy emanating from the ethnic-Hungarian population living in Transylvania (Romania) .

The Romanian Supreme Defense Council has stated that the Szekler autonomy proposal is unconstitutional, 22 January 2004.A statement issued on 21 January by Romania's Supreme Council for National Defense (CSA7) has reportedly stated that a proposed law on autonomy for lands inhabited by the Szelders Hungarian-minority is "unconstitutional". The statement said administrative autonomy and the safeguarding of national minorities' rights must not be mistakenly interpreted as tantamount to territorial autonomy based on ethnicity. President Ion Iliescu said *CSAT* has taken a principled stand on the issue, but noted that deeper analysis of the draft project approved by the Szekler National Council (CNS in Romanian, *SZNT* in Hungarian) is a task for parliament. Iliescu acknowledged that any group of citizens is entitled to propose legislation, but the constitution entitles parliament alone to approve or reject law proposals. CNS Chairman Jozef Csapo said the council has taken note of the *CSAT* position, but intends to continue pushing the proposal in parliament. Csapo added that *CNS* also intends to submit a proposal to the European Parliament and to the

the ongoing conflict in Iraq NATO's Operation "Display Deterrence" for the defense of Turkey stems from Turkey's fear that an Iraq—without a stable government—will lead to the formation of a new state by the ethnic Kurds in Northern Iraq. They might then, in turn, attempt to annex the southern portion of Turkey with its Kurdish population.[32] Thus, the specter of self-determination as a synonym for statehood persists.

4. Final Remarks

The crisis in Kosovo can lead to the reassessment of the absolutist concept of self-determination. Self-determination for ethnic minorities still seems to be divisive by its very nature since it implies a contest for power, control, and authority. However, if a right to self-determination also meant something less than a legal right to sovereignty, the concept could be viewed as an effective protection against the gross violation of minority rights.[33] The tragic Kosovo experience at the end of the last century should result in a careful reassessment of the role of the United Nations security system in the context of the new mission of NATO and post-Cold War ethnic conflicts.[34]

Parliamentary Assembly of the Council of Europe. See <http://www.csees.net>, The Center for South East European Studies: Romania.

[32]NATO, *NATO Defensive Support to Turkey: Operation "Display Deterrence,"* available at http://www.afsouth.nato.int/operations/NATOTurkey/DisplayDeterrenceFactsheet.htm.

[33]Thomas M. Franck, "Postmodern Tribalism and the Right to Secession", in Brolman *et al., op.cit., 4.*

[34]Dana H. Allin, "Debating Intervention", *NATO Review,* Winter Issue 2002, available at http://www.nato.int/docu/review/2002/issue4/english/art1.html (discussing the impact and importance of the Marshall Plan in the reconstruction and stabilization of the war torn countries of

Turning to the contemporary perspective on the Kosovo experience in the light of the first major armed conflict of the new century in Iraq, it seems clear that ethnic self-determination of the Kurds will play a major role in the coming years. Some specific conditions can already be observed:

(1) the collapse of the central authority in the nation state creates the incentive for oppressed ethnic minorities to fight for ethnic self-determination;

(2) the disintegration of a nation-state can destabilize the international legal order;

Therefore, the international community should

(3) provide effective assistance for the protection of ethnic minorities within the framework of the preservation of the nation-state; and

(4) promote conditions for the development of constitutional democracy and the rule of law since they are the best safeguards for internal ethnic self-determination in the framework of a federal legal system.[35]

Western Europe following World War II, and concluding that such a plan may be needed again to help rebuild places like Iraq).

[35]Law on the Protection of Rights and Freedoms of National Minorities, *Official Gazette of FRY* No.11 of 27 February 2002, available at: http://uniadrion.unibo.it/Justice/Archives/Archives.htm. (regulating the "protection of national minorities from all forms of discrimination in exercising their civil rights and freedoms" and protecting "special rights of minorities to minority self-governance in the fields of education, use of language, media and culture and establish[ing] institutions for fostering the participation of minorities in government and in management of national affairs.").

Printed in the United States
137691LV00006B/1/P